The Birthday Almanac

The Birthday Almanac

written by
Claire Saunders

illustrated by
Alison Czinkota

WIDE EYED EDITIONS

TABLE OF CONTENTS

CHAPTER 3

DID YOU KNOW?: BIRTHDAY TRIVIA

THE DAY YOU WERE BORN

Your birthday is the most special day of the year. But what does it mean? How much do you know about the day you were born? Do you know what your birthstone, birth flower, and Celtic tree sign are, and are you curious to know what they say about you? What does your zodiac sign reveal about your personality—and how can it help you plan the perfect birthday?
Have you ever wondered if you share your birthday with a famous figure or a mind-blowing moment in history?

This book contains everything there is to know about the significance of your birthday and the best ways to mark it.

Read all about your zodiac signs, birthstone, birth symbols, and birth number in the **'All About Me'** chapter.

In the **"Month by Month"** chapter, find out what was happening in the world on the day you were born. Perhaps you share your birthday with the historic day humans first set foot on the Moon... or with a record-breaking pot-bellied pig?

Be inspired to plan the perfect birthday, whether it's yours, your best friend's, or your grandma's! The **"Month by Month"** chapter also offers lots of creative birthday ideas and activities for every zodiac sign to get stuck into, from a fortune-telling birthday cake (perfect for mysterious Scorpios) to recycled wrapping ideas (for planet-loving Capricorns).

Finally, dip into the world of birthday trivia in the **"Did You Know?"** chapter, where you can discover lots of curious and crazy facts about birthdays past and present, all around the world.

CHAPTER 1

ALL ABOUT ME: ZODIACS & BIRTH SYMBOLS

What does the day you were born on say about you? Are you a clever Rat or an adventurous Tiger? Is your Celtic tree sign an ambitious Birch or a perceptive Willow? What is your Life Path number and what dream job might it lead you to? Find out all about your zodiac signs, birthstone, birth symbols, and birth number, and discover what they reveal about your personality, strengths, and friendships.

ZODIAC SIGNS

Astrologists believe that your personality is influenced by the position of the planets and stars on the day you were born. Read on to find out what your zodiac sign says about you.

EARTH, AIR, FIRE, WATER

The 12 zodiac signs are divided into four categories:

EARTH signs are down-to-earth, determined, and loyal.

AIR signs are smart, curious, and idealistic.

FIRE signs are enthusiastic, creative, and brave.

WATER signs are emotional, sensitive, and kind.

ON THE CUSP

If you were born on the first or last day of a zodiac sign, that means you were "born on the cusp" and might show characteristics from two zodiac signs—for example, someone born on January 19th might show a mix of Capricorn and Aquarius qualities.

CAPRICORN
The Goat
(December 22nd–January 19th)

COLORS: Brown and black
DAY: Saturday

Capricorns are intelligent, hard-working, and ambitious. They are determined to succeed, and will try again and again until they reach their goal. They love their family and are loyal and dependable, which makes them wonderful friends. Capricorns love to be in nature. They have a special connection with the Earth and care about protecting it.

AQUARIUS
The Water Carrier
(January 20th–February 18th)

COLOR: Light blue
DAY: Wednesday
Unconventional, independent, and adventurous—that's an Aquarius! Discovering new things is their passion. They are clever and curious, and idealistic too—they don't just want to explore the world, they want to make it better. People born under the Aquarius sign are never short of friends. Their charm and charisma mean they get on with everyone.

PISCES
The Fish
(February 19th–March 20th)

COLORS: Light green and lavender
DAY: Thursday
Pisces are so effortlessly cool they don't even realize it! They are happy in their own company, and are completely unbothered by what other people think of them. They are also sensitive and caring, and will help anyone, anywhere, at any time. You'll often find a Pisces making art or writing, or losing themselves in music. They are very intelligent, and have wonderful imaginations.

ARIES
The Ram
(March 21st–April 19th)

COLOR: Red
DAY: Tuesday
Trailblazing Aries like to be first and best at everything—and they generally are! They are full of energy and confidence, and never sit still for long. If there's an adventure to be had, or a challenge to be won, Aries will be first in line. Aries love to be around other people, and will make friends with anyone and everyone. Their warmth and enthusiasm make them brilliant fun to be around.

TAURUS
The Bull
(April 20th–May 20th)

COLORS: Pink and green
DAY: Friday
People born under the sign of Taurus are steady, reliable, and sweet. They love their family and will stay close to their childhood friends for life. Taurus are creatures of habit—they like spending time with the people they know, in the places they know, doing the things that they normally do. Many Taureans are very creative and make wonderful artists or designers. They also love being active.

GEMINI
The Twins
(May 21st–June 21st)

COLOR: Yellow
DAY: Wednesday
Sunny-tempered Geminis are social butterflies, and are always making new friends—they LOVE to chat! It's no wonder they're popular—they're smart, funny, and full of energy, and they always look on the bright side of life. Although Geminis love to be around other people, they're also happy in their own company. They have rich imaginations, and love to write.

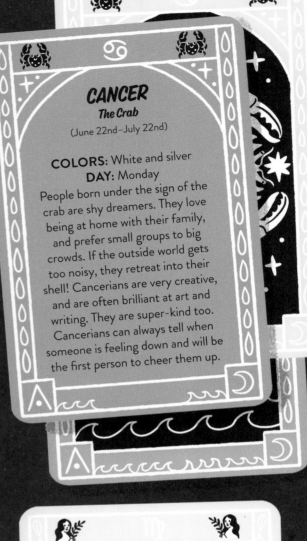

CANCER
The Crab
(June 22nd–July 22nd)

COLORS: White and silver
DAY: Monday
People born under the sign of the crab are shy dreamers. They love being at home with their family, and prefer small groups to big crowds. If the outside world gets too noisy, they retreat into their shell! Cancerians are very creative, and are often brilliant at art and writing. They are super-kind too. Cancerians can always tell when someone is feeling down and will be the first person to cheer them up.

LEO
The Lion
(July 23rd–August 22nd)

COLOR: Gold
DAY: Sunday
Confident and charismatic, Leos are the king of the zodiac jungle. Warm-hearted, funny, and full of energy, they make wonderful friends, and are natural-born leaders. If there's any fun going on, a Leo will be right in the thick of it—they hate to miss out! Leos are also self-confident and determined. There is simply nothing that a Leo can't achieve once they set their mind to it.

VIRGO
The Virgin
(August 23rd– September 22nd)

COLORS: Green and brown
DAY: Wednesday
Virgos are one of the kindest and most caring of all zodiac signs. They love to help others, and they make amazing friends—a Virgo friendship is for life. Practical and organized, they like things to be perfect—you wouldn't catch a Virgo handing in a scruffy piece of half-finished homework! Virgos have a gift with words, and are often talented writers or communicators.

LIBRA
The Scales
(September 23rd–October 23rd)

COLOR: Blue
DAY: Friday

Libra's symbol is a pair of scales, so it's no surprise that balance and harmony are important to them. Libras are natural peacemakers, always the first to sort out any arguments between friends. They are peaceful, generous, and sweet-natured, and are happiest in small groups. Librans often have a gift for words, and they love to be surrounded by beautiful things.

SCORPIO
The Scorpion
(October 24th–November 21st)

COLOR: Black and dark red
DAY: Tuesday

Scorpios are the most mysterious of the zodiac signs—some people even think they have spooky psychic abilities! They are definitely very perceptive, and will notice things that other people don't. Scorpios are very passionate about the things that are important to them, and believe in fairness and honesty. They are also super-smart, independent and very determined—don't ever stand in a Scorpio's way!

SAGITTARIUS
The Archer
(November 22nd–December 21st)

COLOR: Purple
DAY: Thursday

People born under the Sagittarius sign are intrepid and adventurous. They love to try new things and explore other countries and cultures. Energetic and enthusiastic, Sagittarians always have a smile on their face—some people say they are the happiest sign of the zodiac! They have a big heart, and make new friends wherever they go.

FRIEND OR FOE?

Which zodiac signs get on best? And which ones really annoy each other?

Purple: Best friends for life
Yellow: Fun everyday friends
Blue: We don't mind each other
Pink: We're too different to be friends
Green: Uh oh—avoid at all costs!

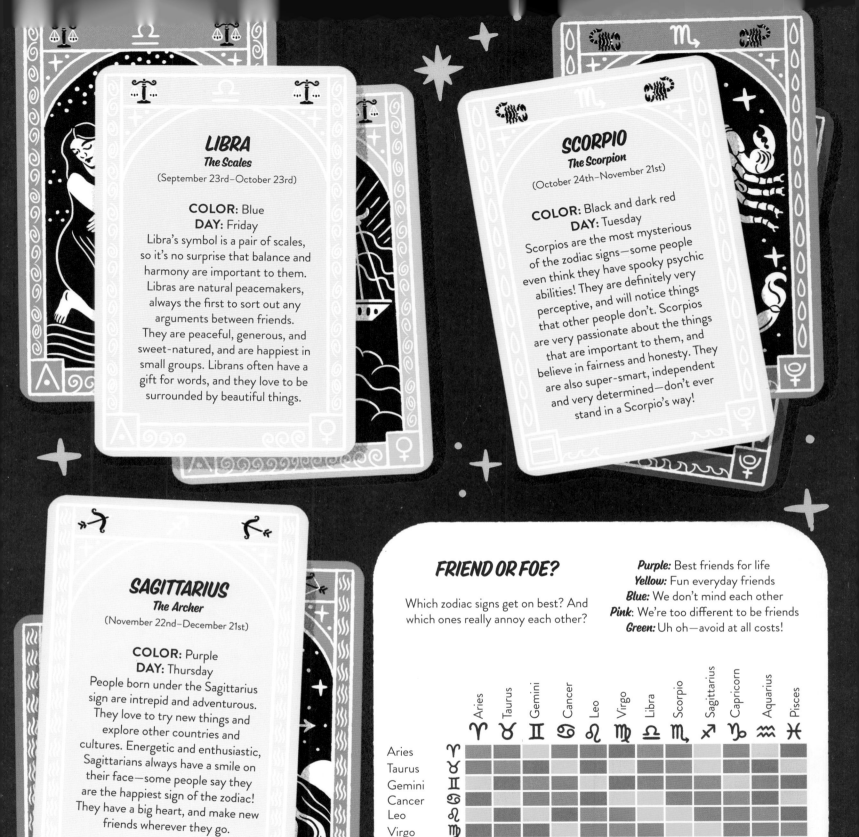

THE CHINESE ZODIAC

The Chinese have their own zodiac, which is based on the year (rather than the month) you were born. There are 12 Chinese zodiac animals, all with their own personalities— do you think your animal sounds like you?

FIRE
Red

Season: Summer
Characteristics: Adventurous and enthusiastic

WOOD
Green

Season: Spring
Characteristics: Creative and brilliant

EARTH
Yellow

Season: Change of seasons
Characteristics: Kind and down-to-earth

Did you know that in Chinese astrology everyone has an element as well as a zodiac animal? To find out which element is yours, first find your zodiac animal. Then check the color of the year you were born and match it to the elements on this page. For example, if you are a Rat born in 2008, your element is Earth (yellow).

WATER
Black

Season: Winter
Characteristics: Sensitive and perceptive

METAL
White

Season: Fall
Characteristics: Ambitious and determined

RAT

*1936, 1948, 1960, **1972**, 1984, 1996, 2008, **2020***

LUCKY HOURS: 11pm to 1am

Quick-witted Rats are clever and determined, so are generally very successful in life. They hate to be bored.

Have fun with

OX, DRAGON, MONKEY

Stay away from

HORSE, ROOSTER

OX

*1937, 1949, 1961, **1973**, 1985, 1997, 2009, **2021***

LUCKY HOURS: 1am to 3am

People born in an Ox year are dependable and hard-working—an Ox will keep going until the job is done. They are also loyal and kind.

Have fun with

SNAKE, ROOSTER, RAT

Stay away from

DRAGON, GOAT

TIGER

*1938, 1950, **1962**, 1974, 1986, 1998, 2010, **2022***

LUCKY HOURS: 3am to 5am

Tigers are confident, enthusiastic, and adventurous. They like to be the best at everything—and they like to show off about it too!

Have fun with

DRAGON, HORSE, DOG

Stay away from

SNAKE, MONKEY

RABBIT

*1939, 1951, **1963**, 1975, 1987, 1999, 2011, **2023***

LUCKY HOURS: 5am to 7am

Rabbits are quiet, kind, and gentle—they rarely lose their temper, and are nice to everyone. Rabbits are also very creative and love beautiful things.

Have fun with

DOG, PIG, GOAT

Stay away from

ROOSTER

DRAGON

1940, 1952, 1964, 1976, 1988, 2000 2012, 2024

LUCKY HOURS: 7am to 9am

Dragons like to be in the center of things and have BIG personalities—they are charismatic, outgoing, and enthusiastic. If a Dragon wants something, they'll get it!

Have fun with

SNAKE, MONKEY, RAT, TIGER

Stay away from

OX, DOG

SNAKE

1941, 1953, 1965, 1977, 1989, 2001 2013, 2025

LUCKY HOURS: 9am to 11am

Snakes are thinkers. They are very wise and intelligent, but are also quite private—they don't like to reveal what they're thinking. Snakes are also stylish, and love luxury.

Have fun with

ROOSTER, DRAGON, OX

Stay away from

TIGER

HORSE

1942, 1954, 1966, 1978, 1990, 2002, 2014, 2026

LUCKY HOURS: 11am to 1pm

Horses are easy-going, positive people with loads of energy. They're often found in a big crowd of friends—they love to be around people having fun.

Have fun with

GOAT, DOG, TIGER

Stay away from

RAT

GOAT

1943, 1955, 1967, 1979, 1991, 2003, 2015, 2027

LUCKY HOURS: 1pm to 3pm

Kind-hearted Goats are shy and gentle, and don't like to be the center of attention. They are often very artistic and creative.

Have fun with

PIG, RABBIT, HORSE

Stay away from

OX

MONKEY

1944, 1956, 1968, 1980,
1992, 2004, 2016, 2028

LUCKY HOURS: 3pm to 5pm

Monkeys are super-smart! They want to know EVERYTHING, and pick things up quickly. Their fun, mischievous personalities make them very popular.

Have fun with
RAT, DRAGON

Stay away from
PIG, TIGER

ROOSTER

1945, 1957, 1969, 1981,
1993, 2005, 2017, 2029

LUCKY HOURS: 5pm to 7pm

Outgoing and confident, Roosters enjoy the spotlight, and love to chat and tell jokes. They're also perfectionists—only the best will do for a Rooster!

Have fun with
OX, SNAKE

Stay away from
RAT, RABBIT

DOG

1946, 1958, 1970, 1982,
1994, 2006, 2018, 2030

LUCKY HOURS: 7pm to 9pm

Everyone loves a Dog! Not only are they playful and fun, but they are also incredibly loyal. They will always be there for their friends, and stand up for what's right.

Have fun with
PIG, TIGER, RABBIT, HORSE

Stay away from
DRAGON

PIG

1947, 1959, 1971, 1983,
1995, 2007, 2019, 2031

LUCKY HOURS: 9pm to 11pm

Warm, sunny-tempered, and generous, Pigs make wonderful friends. They love their creature comforts and snuggling up at home with their family.

Have fun with
RABBIT, GOAT, DOG

Stay away from
MONKEY

BIRTHSTONES

Every month has its own gemstone, each with its own special meaning. Some people think that wearing these gemstones brings them luck, and people have even believed that wearing them gives superpowers, such as seeing into the future or becoming invisible.

JANUARY
Garnet

Most people think of garnets as red, but they come in lots of other colors too. Some even change color, depending on the light. Magic!

Wealth

Health

Everlasting friendship

FEBRUARY
Amethyst

Courage

Inner strength

Calmness

Amethysts were once as valuable as diamonds, and were worn by royalty throughout Europe and Asia.

MARCH
Aquamarine

Youth

Health

Hope

The ancient Greeks and Romans called this beautiful sea-colored stone "the sailor's gem." They believed it kept them safe at sea.

Alternative birthstone:
Bloodstone

APRIL
Diamond

Diamonds are the world's most valuable gemstone, and the hardest substance on Earth. Did you know that the only thing that can scratch a diamond is another diamond?

Everlasting love

MAY
Emerald

Good fortune

Wisdom

Rebirth

Hundreds of years ago, people believed that placing an emerald under your tongue gave you the power to see into the future.

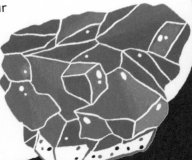

JUNE
Pearl

 Purity

 Innocence

The Egyptian queen Cleopatra used a pearl to win a bet that she could host the world's most expensive dinner—she took off one of her priceless pearl earrings, dissolved it in a glass of wine, and drank it!

Alternative birthstones:
Moonstone, Alexandrite

JULY
Ruby

Success

Good fortune

Love

The ruby is known as the king of precious stones. Historically, rubies were believed to protect against evil and warn of approaching danger by turning darker in color.

AUGUST
Peridot

 Wealth

Power

For centuries, the peridot was used as a protective talisman against evil spirits, nightmares, and enchantments.

Alternative birthstones:
Spinel, Sardonyx

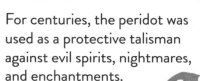

SEPTEMBER
Sapphire

 Loyalty

 Honesty

 Trust

Sapphires were once believed to have healing powers. In the 1500s, King Charles V would touch people's eyes with his sapphire ring to cure them of diseases.

OCTOBER
Opal

Hope

Truth

 Luck

It was once thought that opals could make you invisible—and that they could teleport themselves from one place to another when no one was looking.

Alternative birthstone:
Tourmaline

NOVEMBER
Topaz

Wealth

Health

Calmness

At one time, topaz was thought to attract gold and wealth to its wearer. It is also a sign of love and affection.

Alternative birthstone:
Citrine

DECEMBER
Tanzanite

 Generosity

 Friendship

Tanzanite is found in only one place on the entire planet—in Tanzania, East Africa.

Alternative birthstones:
 Zircon **Turquoise**

BIRTH NUMBERS

Numerology is a type of fortune-telling by numbers! It believes that numbers have special meanings, and that the numbers in your date of birth reveal the talents you were born with.

WORK OUT YOUR LIFE PATH NUMBER

In numerology, one of the most important numbers is a person's "Life Path number." To work out yours, add up all of the separate digits in your date of birth, and keep adding them until you end up with just one number—your Life Path number. Here's an example for someone whose birthday is **NOVEMBER 27TH, 2008.**

MONTH

November is the 11th month of the year. 11 is split into:

$1 + 1$ which adds up to 2

DAY

The day is the 27th. 27 is split into:

$2 + 7$ which adds up to 9

YEAR

The year 2008 is split into

$2+0+0+8$ which adds up to 10 This is then split again: $1+0 = 1$

ADD THE THREE NUMBERS TOGETHER

$2 + 9 + 1 = 12$ This is then split again: $1+2 = 3$

THE LIFE PATH NUMBER IS 3

Ones are natural-born leaders. Strong and determined, they will generally rise to the top in whatever they do. They are unwaveringly loyal to their friends.
Jobs: *Politician, business leader, influencer*

Twos are peacemakers. Balanced and tactful, they always know how to sort out arguments. They are also smart and resilient—whatever challenges they face, they will always bounce back.
Jobs: *Diplomat, politician, judge*

Threes live life to the full! Funny, charming, and charismatic, they love to entertain others and be in the spotlight. Threes are imaginative, and often enjoy working in creative jobs.
Jobs: *Actor, musician, TV presenter*

Down-to-earth Fours are organized and hard-working, and like things to be perfect. Fours often enjoy making things and can be extremely successful in life.
Jobs: *Craftsperson, chef, engineer*

Eights go hand in hand with success and wealth. They are ambitious, risk-taking, and hard-working (sometimes a bit too hard-working!), and they inspire everyone around them.
Jobs: *Entrepreneur, inventor, business leader*

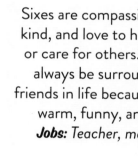

Sixes are compassionate and kind, and love to help, teach, or care for others. Sixes will always be surrounded by friends in life because they are warm, funny, and loyal.
Jobs: *Teacher, medic, vet*

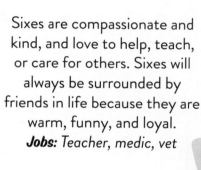

Fives are always on the go and hate to be tied down. Dynamic and smart, they get bored easily, and love new challenges and adventures.
Jobs: *Travel writer, film-maker, astronaut*

Nines want to make the world a better place. When they see suffering or injustice, they can't rest until they have helped. Nines are sensitive souls, and often very artistic.
Jobs: *Journalist, activist, artist*

Imaginative Sevens are thinkers and dreamers—they are constantly seeking knowledge and asking "Why?" In life, they don't care about being rich or popular, and will always be true to themselves.
Jobs: *Scientist, professor, writer*

WHICH FLOWER ARE YOU?

JANUARY
CARNATION, SNOWDROP

Carnation people are kind and loyal, and always there for their friends.

Carnation
admiration, love and loyalty

Snowdrop
hope and beauty

FEBRUARY
VIOLET, PRIMROSE, IRIS

Violet people are observant, thoughtful, and honest.

Violet
loyalty and modesty

Primrose
love

Iris
hope and wisdom

MARCH
DAFFODIL

Sunny daffodil people are happiest when they're with the people they love.

Daffodil
love, rebirth, and good luck

APRIL
DAISY, SWEET PEA

Loyal daisy people are good at keeping their friends' secrets.

Daisy
innocence, loyalty, purity

Sweet pea
happiness and pleasure

MAY
LILY OF THE VALLEY, HAWTHORN

Lily of the valley people are kind and modest—they don't like to boast.

Lily of the Valley
sweetness, purity, and humility

Hawthorn
hope and happiness

JUNE
ROSE, HONEYSUCKLE

Rose people are loving and affectionate.

Rose
love, honor, and beauty

Honeysuckle
happiness and affection

JULY
LARKSPUR, WATERLILY

Larkspur people are optimistic and positive.

Waterlily
purity, majesty, and wisdom

Larkspur
happiness, love, and positivity

Are you a kind carnation, a loyal daisy, or a determined marigold? Read on to find out all about the special meanings of birth month flowers.

Gladiolus
strength of character, generosity, and honor

AUGUST
GLADIOLUS, POPPY

Gladiolus people will stand up for what they believe in.

Poppy
pleasure, success, and imagination

SEPTEMBER
ASTER, MORNING GLORY

Aster people are wise and brave leaders.

Aster
wisdom, bravery, and powerful love

Morning glory
affection and love

OCTOBER
MARIGOLD, COSMOS

Marigold people are gifted and determined and won't give up.

Marigold
determination, wealth, creativity

Cosmos
order, peace, harmony

NOVEMBER
CHRYSANTHEMUM

Chrysanthemum people bring joy into everyone's lives.

Chrysanthemum
loyalty, happiness, and good luck

Holly
protection and hope

DECEMBER
NARCISSUS, HOLLY, POINSETTA

Narcissus people are optimistic and attract good luck.

Poinsetta
cheerfulness and success

Narcissus
hope, wealth, and good fortune

THE CELTIC TREE CALENDAR

Trees were very special to the ancient Celts. People believed that certain trees had special powers or were home to magical spirits and fairies. Much later, particular trees were linked to the 13 lunar (Moon) months. Do you know which tree sign YOU were born under?

HAWTHORN
The Illusionist
(May 13—June 9)

Hawthorns often surprise people—how they appear on the outside can be quite different from how they are on the inside. Hawthorns are very creative and are good listeners.

WILLOW
The Observer
April 15—May 12

Willows are intelligent and perceptive—they often notice things that other people don't. They are also very patient.

ALDER
The Trailblazer
(March 18—April 14)

Alders are confident, charismatic, and popular. They like to lead and get on with everyone.

ASH
The Enchanter
(February 18—March 17)

Ashes are imaginative and artistic, and sometimes get lost in their own dream world. They love writing and making art.

ROWAN
The Thinker
(January 21—February 17)

Rowans are super-creative and bursting with ideas. They can seem quiet, but there is a lot going on in their busy minds.

BIRCH
The Achiever
(December 24—January 20)

Birches are ambitious and determined to succeed. They are charming and funny, and make natural leaders.

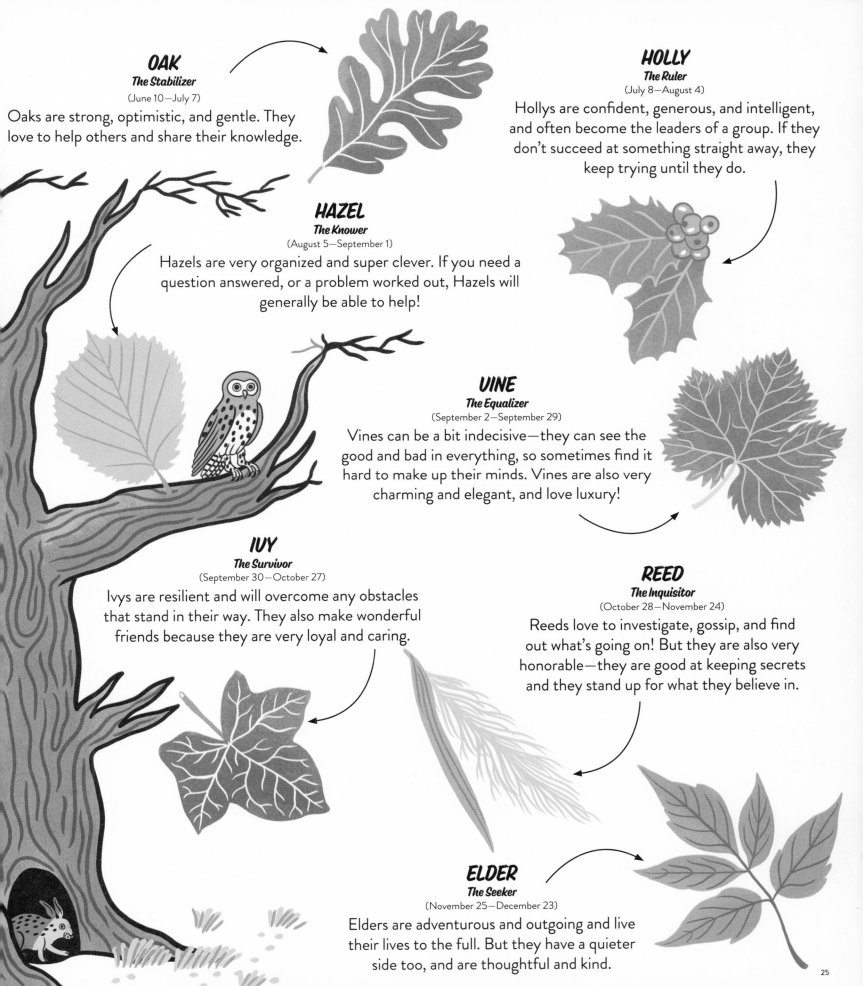

OAK
The Stabilizer
(June 10—July 7)

Oaks are strong, optimistic, and gentle. They love to help others and share their knowledge.

HOLLY
The Ruler
(July 8—August 4)

Hollys are confident, generous, and intelligent, and often become the leaders of a group. If they don't succeed at something straight away, they keep trying until they do.

HAZEL
The Knower
(August 5—September 1)

Hazels are very organized and super clever. If you need a question answered, or a problem worked out, Hazels will generally be able to help!

VINE
The Equalizer
(September 2—September 29)

Vines can be a bit indecisive—they can see the good and bad in everything, so sometimes find it hard to make up their minds. Vines are also very charming and elegant, and love luxury!

IVY
The Survivor
(September 30—October 27)

Ivys are resilient and will overcome any obstacles that stand in their way. They also make wonderful friends because they are very loyal and caring.

REED
The Inquisitor
(October 28—November 24)

Reeds love to investigate, gossip, and find out what's going on! But they are also very honorable—they are good at keeping secrets and they stand up for what they believe in.

ELDER
The Seeker
(November 25—December 23)

Elders are adventurous and outgoing and live their lives to the full. But they have a quieter side too, and are thoughtful and kind.

25

MONDAY TO SUNDAY BIRTHDAYS

Which day of the week were you born, and what does it say about you?

Did you know that the ancient Romans named the days of the week after their gods and goddesses and the planets they were associated with? Each god has a distinct personality, and so does each day.

MONDAY
The Moon
People born on the day of the Moon goddess are kind, gentle, and sensitive. They love to be surrounded by their friends and family.

TUESDAY
Mars
Tuesdays are associated with Mars, the Roman god of war and battle. Like him, people born on this day are fiery, energetic, and courageous, and never, ever give up.

THURSDAY
Jupiter
Thursdays belong to the king of the gods, Jupiter—the god of thunder and lightning. People born on this day are charismatic and full of energy, and love fun and adventure.

WEDNESDAY
Mercury
People born on a Wednesday are influenced by Mercury, the messenger of the gods. They are quick-witted and great at communicating with others, and they love to explore new places.

SUNDAY
The Sun

Lucky you if you were born on a Sunday. Like the Sun god, you are bright and dazzling, and you shine your cheerful, optimistic warmth on everyone you meet.

FRIDAY
Venus

Friday people are born under the influence of Venus, the goddess of love and beauty. They are affectionate, creative, and elegant, and love to be loved.

SATURDAY
Saturn

Saturdays are associated with Saturn, the god of wealth and plenty. People born on this day are smart, hard-working, and responsible.

MONDAY'S CHILD

You might already have heard this old fortune-telling rhyme. Whether or not you believe in it might depend on which day of the week you were born on—nobody really wants to be a miserable Wednesday's child, do they?

Monday's child is fair of face
Tuesday's child is full of grace
Wednesday's child is full of woe
Thursday's child has far to go
Friday's child is loving and giving
Saturday's child works hard for a living
But the child who is born on the Sabbath day
Is bonnie and blithe and good and gay.

CHAPTER 2

MONTH BY MONTH: CALENDARS & ACTIVITIES

What was happening in the world on the dates that you and your friends were born? Flip through these calendars to find out. Perhaps you share your birthday with a great artist, an inspiring activist, or an eminent genius. Maybe a great book, film, or song was released, a momentous historical event took place, or an amazing world record was broken. You might even be lucky enough to share your birthday with World Chocolate Day (yum)!

After each calendar month, there are birthday-themed activities for every zodiac sign—party-planner quizzes for outgoing Geminis, crafty decorations for creative Taureans, and birthday bake gifts for kind and thoughtful Virgos. Some of the activities can be used to plan your birthday, while others are fun ideas for making other people's birthdays extra-special. Learn how to become a present-wrapping maestro, plan a balloon ambush for an unsuspecting grown-up, whip up some fizz-popping mocktails for your party, and much more!

25

Today is Burns Night in Scotland, held in honor of poet Robert Burns. The traditional celebration features bagpipers and the Scottish dish haggis.

JANUARY

What was happening in the world on the day you were born? Let's find out.

Garnet
BIRTHSTONE

Carnation and snowdrop
BIRTH FLOWERS

Dec 22–Jan 19
CAPRICORN

Jan 20–Feb 18
AQUARIUS

01 Today is **New Year's Day!** If you stay up late on New Year's Eve, you can start celebrating your birthday at 1 second past midnight.

02 In 1860, Frenchman Urbain Le Verrier announced he'd discovered a new planet, Vulcan. It took 55 years to prove it didn't exist after all.

03 You share your birthday with Greta Thunberg, the Swedish schoolgirl and climate activist.

04 In 2019, Matthieu Tordeur (age 27) became the youngest person to reach the South Pole on a solo trek.

05 It's Twelfth Night, the last night of the Twelve Days of Christmas. The traditional Twelfth Night cake has a bean baked into it—whoever finds it gets good luck.

06 Today is the birthday of the famous fictional detective Sherlock Holmes.

07 On this day in 1950, the song Rudolph the Red-nosed Reindeer was No. 1 in the US pop charts.

08 You share your birthday with Elvis Presley, the king of rock and roll, and brainy physicist Stephen Hawking.

09 The record for the most party poppers popped in a minute—a whopping 78—was set today in 2016.

10 The first *Adventures of Tinton* comic book, written by Belgian cartoonist Hergé, was published today in 1929.

11 In 1838, the very first message was sent using the dots and dashes that became known as Morse Code.

12 Today in 1967, James Bedford became the first human to be cryonically frozen after he died, in the hope that he could be cured and "woken up" in the future.

13 You share your birthday with American Impressionist painter Lilla Cabot Perry.

14 **Happy Old New Year!** Under the old Julian calendar (which was used until 1582), today was New Year's Day.

15 You share your birthday with American civil rights activist Martin Luther King Jr.

16 Ellen Johnson Sirleaf became Africa's first female head of state, when she was elected President of Liberia in 2006.

17 Roald Dahl's *Charlie and the Chocolate Factory* was published today in 1964.

18 Today is **Winnie-the-Pooh Day!** The much-loved bear was created by English author A. A. Milne, who was born today in 1882.

19 Get popping—it's **National Popcorn Day in the USA.**

20 In 2009, Barack Obama was sworn in as America's first black president.

21 Concorde took its very first flight today in 1976. The supersonic planes stopped flying in 2003.

22 The planet's fastest-ever temperature change took place today in 1943, in Spearfish, South Dakota. It rose 49 °F in just two minutes.

23 The first dive to the bottom of the Mariana Trench (the deepest point on Earth) took place today, in 1960.

24 In America, today is **National Compliment Day.** Why don't you compliment the next person you see?

25 (see opposite page)

26 The Cullinan Diamond (the largest ever found) was discovered in South Africa in 1905.

27 You share your birthday with Lewis Carroll, author of *Alice in Wonderland*, and composer Wolfgang Amadeus Mozart.

28 The first Lego brick was patented today, in 1958.

29 German Carl Benz created the design for the first modern car today, in 1886.

30 Ernő Rubik applied for a patent for his "Magic Cube" —the Rubik's Cube—in 1975.

31 Today is **Backwards Day,** when you get to do everything... backwards. Wear your clothes inside-out, walk backwards, and eat breakfast in the evening.

JUNK MAIL GIFT BOW

You wouldn't think you could turn boring junk mail into something beautiful, but you can! This recycled gift bow looks amazing and is eco-friendly, too—perfect for considerate CAPRICORNS, who care about the planet.

YOU WILL NEED:

- Junk mail leaflets, old magazines, or catalogs
- A ruler
- Scissors
- Stapler
- Double-sided sticky tape or glue

1. First, choose the magazine pages or junk mail that you want to use. Look for bright colors and patterns.

2. Cut up your paper up into strips ¾ in. wide. You will need 3 long strips of paper (around 11 in. long); 3 slightly shorter strips (around 10 in. long); and 1 short strip (around 2½ in. long).

3. To begin, take one of the longest strips and loop one end of it over.

X3 X3 X1

Make sure you keep the brightest side of the paper on the outside.

4. Turn the strip the other way up, and make a loop at the other end in exactly the same way as you did the first one. Then staple both ends in place. This can be a bit fiddly—get an adult to help you with the first strip if you need to. You'll soon get the hang of it!

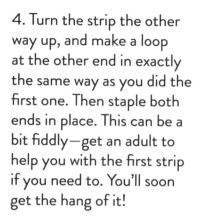

5. Repeat with the other two long strips. Then do the same thing with your three shorter strips.

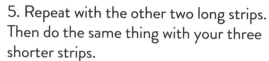

6. Now you can begin to assemble your bow! Position your three larger loops one on top of each other, attaching them with sticky tape or glue.

7. Next stick your three small smaller loops on top of the larger loops.

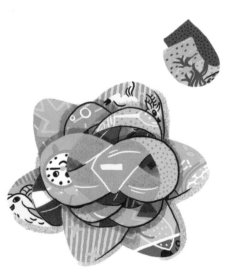

8. To finish your bow, roll up your very smallest strip of paper into a small cylinder and stick it into the center.

OTHER RECYCLED WRAPPING IDEAS

• Use pages torn out of old comics to wrap a friend's present.
• Wrap a present in a sheet of old newspaper—and highlight individual letters or words to spell out a secret birthday message!
• Use your old pictures and paintings as wrapping paper.
• Turn a toilet roll tube into a gift box. Paint or decorate it, push in the ends, and tie it with a ribbon to hold everything in place (see below).

FEBRUARY

What was happening in the world on the day you were born? Let's find out.

Amethyst
BIRTHSTONE

Violet, Iris, and Primrose
BIRTH FLOWERS

Jan 20–Feb 18
AQUARIUS

Feb 19–March 20
PISCES

01 You share your birthday with *Imbolc*, an ancient Celtic celebration that marked the beginning of spring.

02 Today is *Groundhog Day* in the US, when crowds gather to watch a groundhog come out of its burrow and predict the weather.

03 In 1966, the unmanned Soviet Luna 9 became the first spaceship to make a controlled landing on the Moon.

04 Facebook was launched today in 2004 by 19-year-old Mark Zuckerberg and his college roommates.

05 The biggest gold nugget in history (named the "Welcome Stranger") was found today, in 1869. It weighed around 70 kg.

06 You share your birthday with Jamaican reggae musician Bob Marley.

07 Today in 2005, Ellen MacArthur sailed around the world by herself in a record time—71 days.

08 You share your birthday with American surfer Bethany Harrison. She lost her arm to a shark when she was 13, but went on to become a champion surfer.

09 Volleyball was invented today, in 1895.

10 The first Tom and Jerry cartoon was shown today in 1940.

11 In 1990, Nelson Mandela was released from prison, after 27 years as a political prisoner. He later became president of South Africa.

12 Today is *Darwin Day*, celebrating the birth of Charles Darwin and his ground-breaking ideas on evolution.

13 In 2004, the biggest diamond in the Universe was discovered, in a star 50 light-years away from Earth.

14 Today is *Valentine's Day*, a celebration of love. Maybe you'll get a Valentine's card along with your birthday cards.

15 You share your birthday with the great Antarctic explorer, Ernest Shackleton.

16 Today in 1923, the burial chamber of Egyptian Pharaoh Tutankhamun was opened, unleashing the "Curse of Tutankhamun."

17 Today is *Random Acts of Kindness Day* in the USA—why don't YOU do a kind act today?

18 Pluto (once believed to be the ninth planet in our solar system) was discovered today, in 1930.

19 In 1986, Russia launched the Mir space station into orbit.

20 The first performance of Tchaikovsky's *Swan Lake* ballet took place today, in 1877 (see opposite page).

21 You share your birthday with American jazz legend Nina Simone and English-American poet W.H. Auden.

22 Today in 2001 German Jan Hempel set a record for the longest backwards jump from standing: 6 feet and 7 inches.

23 The famous Gutenberg Bible was published today, in 1455. It was the first book to be printed using moveable type.

24 The world's first opera, Claudio Monteverdi's *L'Orfeo*, was performed in 1607.

25 You share your birthday with Impressionist painter Pierre Renoir, and lead guitarist of The Beatles, George Harrison.

26 The first color film was shown to the public today in 1909, in London.

27 In 1932, English scientist James Chadwick discovered the neutron—one of the tiny particles that make up atoms.

28 In 2016, Aleix Segura Vendrell from Spain held his breath underwater for over 24 minutes, breaking the world record.

29 Happy Birthday leaplings. Your birthday is pretty special—the chance of being born on this day is just 1 in 1,461.

FUROSHIKI WRAPPING

If you're an AQUARIUS, you are curious about the world, and love to discover new things. Did you know that in Japan presents are sometimes wrapped not in paper, but in material instead? Furoshiki wrapping is a Japanese artform, and now you can learn how to do it too.

WHAT'S A FUROSHIKI?

A furoshiki is a piece of beautiful cloth that is used to wrap and carry things. These helpful little squares of fabric have been used in Japan for over 1,200 years, and can be used not only to wrap gifts, but also to carry food and shopping. They come in lots of different sizes, and can be tied lots of different ways.

One of the great things about furoshiki wrapping (apart from it looking amazing of course) is that it can be used again and again, and so is kind to the planet.

MAKING FUROSHIKI

You can buy furoshiki online, but it's more fun to make your own. Ask your grown-ups if they have any old scraps of fabric lying about, or look out for bright, patterned fabric in second-hand shops—thin scarfs or large handkerchiefs are perfect.

Old, worn-out sheets, or pillowcases are also brilliant. Ask your grown-up if you can cut one up, and then decorate it using fabric pens or paints.

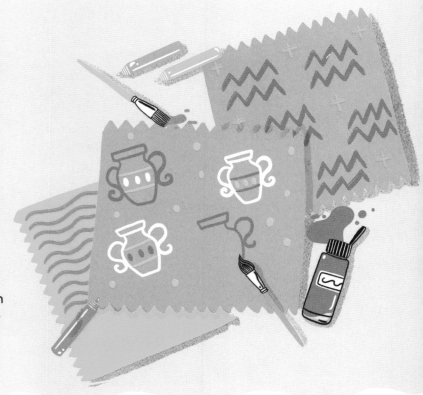

To make a furoshiki that's big enough to wrap a small book, you will need to cut your fabric into a square that's about 20 in. by 20 in.. Use pinking shears to trim the edges of your fabric, to stop it from fraying. Bigger presents will need a larger-sized furoshiki.

Here are two different ways to fold and tie your furoshiki. You can find lots more online.

The nice thing about giving someone a furoshiki-wrapped present is that they will be able to re-use the furoshiki themselves. Make sure you give them some instructions on how to tie it, or a quick demonstration. How many presents do you think your furoshiki might end up wrapping? One day it might even come all the way back to you.

OTSUKAI TSUTSUMI (BASIC WRAP)

1. Lay out the furoshiki and place the present in the center, at a diagonal. Fold the top-right corner of the cloth towards you.

2. Fold the opposite corner away from you.

3. Grab the other two corners, and tie them together in a knot.

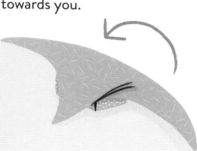

YOTSU MUSUBI (FOUR TIE WRAP)

1. Lay out the furoshiki and place the present in the center, at a diagonal.

2. Grab the top-left and bottom-right corners, and tie them together in a knot.

3. Tie the other two corners together.

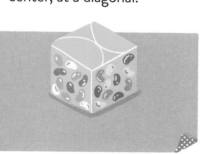
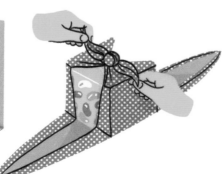

BRILLIANT BIRTHDAY BRIGADEIROS

In Brazil, no children's birthday party is complete without brigadeiros—small balls of chocolatey deliciousness covered with an explosion of sprinkles. If you're an adventurous AQUARIUS, who loves to try out new things, why not make some for a friend or parent's birthday?

This recipe makes about 20 brigadeiros.

YOU WILL NEED:

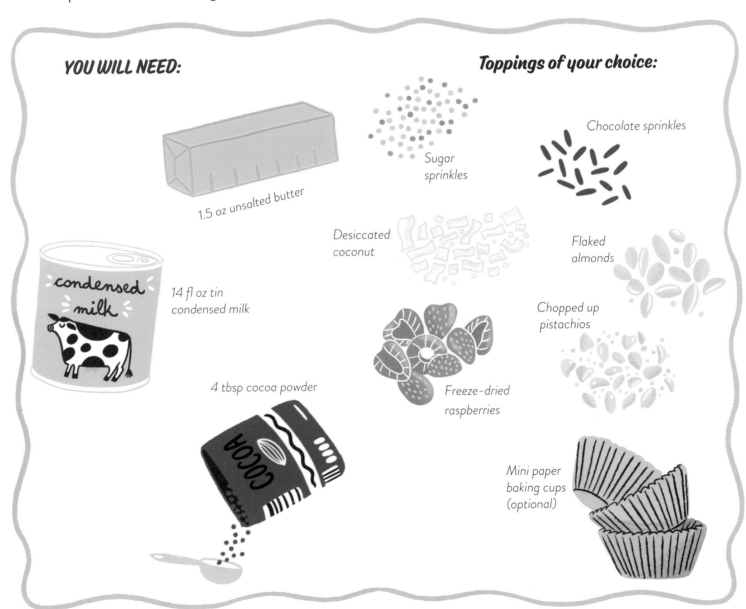

1.5 oz unsalted butter

14 fl oz tin condensed milk

4 tbsp cocoa powder

Toppings of your choice:

Sugar sprinkles

Chocolate sprinkles

Desiccated coconut

Flaked almonds

Chopped up pistachios

Freeze-dried raspberries

Mini paper baking cups (optional)

HOW TO MAKE THEM:

1 In a saucepan, heat the butter, condensed milk, and cocoa powder, stirring with a wooden spoon, until the mixture starts to boil. Reduce the heat and cook for 10 minutes, stirring constantly, until the mixture is thick and glossy.

TIP
You can tell your mixture is ready when you can briefly see the bottom of the pan when you scrape it with your spoon.

2 Remove the pan from the heat and set aside to cool until the mixture is cool enough to be handled. This will take at least two hours, so you will need to be patient...

3 Now for the messy bit! Once the mixture is completely cool, tip your chosen toppings into small bowls, then butter your hands. Scoop up small amounts of the mixture and roll them into balls between your hands, then roll them through a topping so they're completely covered. Place them into mini baking cups or on a plate lined with greaseproof paper.

TIP
If the mixture is too squidgy and sticky to form into balls, pop it into the fridge to set for half an hour.

Your brigadeiros can be stored in a tin or other container for up to 2 days, or in the fridge for 4–7 days. They're tastiest eaten at room temperature.

Take care when you are heating the chocolate mixture. Always ask an adult for help and advice.

31

On this day in 1889, Paris's iconic Eiffel Tower opened.

MARCH

What was happening in the world on the day you were born? Let's find out.

Aquamarine
BIRTHSTONE

Daffodil
BIRTH FLOWER

Feb 19–March 20
PISCES

March 21–April 19
ARIES

01 Today in 1872, Yellowstone in the US became the world's first national park.

02 *The Sound of Music* film was released today, in 1965.

03 You share your birthday with *World Wildlife Day*.

04 "Happy Birthday to you, Happy Birthday to you!" The Happy Birthday song was published today in 1924!

05 Today in 2019 Bugatti unveiled La Voiture Noire—the most expensive supercar ever. It cost almost $19 million, and only one was ever made.

06 On this day in 1869, Russian chemist Dmitri Mendeleev presented his periodic table of chemical elements.

07 In 1876, Alexander Graham Bell was awarded the first patent for a telephone.

08 Today is *International Women's Day*, which celebrates women and fights for their rights around the world.

09 In 1959, the first Barbie went on sale.

10 The first telephone call was made today, in 1876, to someone in the next door room!

11 You share your birthday with British writer Douglas Adams, author of *The Hitchhiker's Guide to the Galaxy*.

12 Dr Seuss's *The Cat in the Hat* was published today in 1957.

13 The planet Uranus was discovered today, in 1781, by astronomer William Herschel.

14 You share your birthday with scientific genius Albert Einstein.

15 In ancient Rome in 44 BCE, Julius Caesar was assassinated by a group of senators.

16 In 1900, the ancient city of Knossos—site of the legendary minotaur's labyrinth—was rediscovered in Crete.

17 Wear something green today—it's *St. Patrick's Day*, a celebration of all things Irish!

18 In 1965, Russian cosmonaut Aleksei Leonov became the first person to walk in space.

19 The Sydney Harbour Bridge opened today, in 1932.

20 Today is *International Day of Happiness*—the perfect day to have a birthday!

21 You share your birthday with *World Poetry Day*. Why not read (or write) a poem today?

22 The pop band The Beatles released their first album, *Please Please Me*, today, in 1963.

23 You share your birthday with British athlete Roger Bannister, who in 1954 became the first person to run a mile in under 4 minutes.

24 You share your birthday with magician Harry Houdini, who was famous for his incredible escape acts.

25 Today is *International Tolkien Reading Day*. Have you read any of his books?

26 On this day in 2012, James Cameron made the first solo dive to Challenger Deep—the deepest point of the ocean.

27 Draw back the curtains and take a bow—today is *World Theater Day*.

28 You share your birthday with American musician and actress Lady Gaga.

29 Today in 1974, the famous Terracotta Army—a collection of 8,000 life-size statues—was discovered in Xi'an, China.

30 You share your birthday with famous painter Vincent Van Gogh.

31 see opposite page

WRAP IT UP

Are you a kind-hearted, creative PISCES who loves to make other people's birthdays special? If so, here are some wrapping ideas that make the opening of a present just as exciting as the gift inside.

THE GREAT PRESENT HUNT

This birthday treasure hunt needs a bit of preparation, lots and lots of wool, and grown-ups who don't mind their home being transformed into an obstacle course.

First, wrap up the present and hide it somewhere in the house. Take a large ball of wool and tie one end of the wool to the present. Now the fun starts. Holding the ball of wool, walk around the house, unraveling the wool as you go. Wind it several times around door knobs, bannisters, lampshades, chair legs, and other bits of furniture, high up and low down, until the wool is all used up. If you want to make your trail longer, you can join two balls of wool together.

Hand the end of the ball of wool to the birthday person, and tell them they need to follow the trail to find their present. They will need to be prepared to do lots of ninja-style ducking under and climbing over the wool as they follow the trail to the very end.

It's up to you how long or short or difficult you make the trail.

PASS THE PARCEL PRESENT

Unwrapping is so much fun that there's a whole children's party game devoted to it. In Pass the Parcel, a prize is wrapped in several layers of wrapping paper. The parcel is passed from one child to another, and whoever is holding it when the music stops removes a layer of wrapping. The child who removes the final layer of paper wins the prize.

You can create your own Pass the Parcel Birthday Present for someone special by wrapping their present in lots of different layers—and letting them open ALL the layers themselves for maximum fun. Use old wrapping paper, newspaper, tissue paper, or even some of your old drawings. Just make sure each layer of paper has a different design.

To make the parcel extra-special, add a small surprise to each layer. This could be...
•a chocolate or piece of candy
•a favorite photograph of you and the birthday person
•a challenge that they have to complete before they unwrap the next layer
•a note telling them why you love them
•a joke to make them laugh
•an instruction for how they should open the next layer—for example, using only one hand, or their teeth.

For a final challenge, wrap the very last layer using LOADS of sticky tape to make it super-difficult to open.

APRIL

What was happening in the world on the day you were born? Let's find out.

Diamond
BIRTHSTONE

Daisy and Sweet pea
BIRTH FLOWERS

March 21–April 19
ARIES

April 20–May 20
TAURUS

01 *April Fools' Day!*
All sorts of jokes, hoaxes, and general silliness are allowed today!

02 Today is *Tailie Day* in Scotland. Traditionally, jokers stuck paper tails onto people's bottoms.

03 On this day in 1973, the first ever mobile phone call was made, from a pavement in New York City.

04 The American writer and activist Maya Angelou was born in 1928.

05 The real-life Pocohontas, daughter of an Indian chief, married tobacco planter John Rolfe in Virginia, USA, in 1614.

06 This may—or may not—have been the day when Robert Peary became the first person to reach the North Pole, in 1909. Not everyone believed him.

07 Today is the symbolic birth date of the internet. The very first ideas about how it could work were shared today in 1969.

08 The birth of Gautama Buddha, the founder of Buddhism, is celebrated today. He's thought to have lived in India from 563 to 483 BCE.

09 The first-known recording of the human voice (singing the French song *Au clair de la lune*) took place today, in 1860.

10 Today is *Siblings Day* in the US. It's a time to celebrate and honor your brothers and sisters—but don't tell them that.

11 Today, Halley's Comet came closest to Earth on its 1986 visit. It won't return until 2061—how old will you be?

12 Soviet cosmonaut Yuri Gagarin became the first human in space in 1961 (see opposite page).

13 In 1997, 21-year-old Tiger Woods became the youngest ever golfer to win the Masters Tournament.

14 On this day in 1912, just before midnight, the ocean liner *Titanic* struck an iceberg in the North Atlantic. It sank a few hours later.

15 Leonardo da Vinci, the Italian painter, sculptor, architect, and all-round genius, was born today in 1452.

16 Hollywood legend Charlie Chaplin was born on this day in 1889.

17 Today is *International Haiku Poetry Day*.
Haiku are short Japanese poems just 17 syllables long.

18 You share your birthday with Scottish actor David Tennant and reality TV star Kourtney Kardashian.

19 The American Revolution began in Lexington, Massachusetts, in 1775. It ended eight years later with independence from Great Britain.

20 In 1902, scientist Marie Curie and her husband Pierre discovered the radioactive element radium.

21 Henry VIII—famous for his six wives—was crowned King of England today, in 1509.

22 It's *Earth Day*
People around the world show support for protecting the environment.

23 The first-ever YouTube video (an 18-second clip of San Diego zoo) was uploaded today, in 2014.

24 The Hubble Space Telescope was launched into space in 1990. It allowed scientists to see far-away stars and galaxies for the first time.

25 Jazz legend Ella Fitzgerald was born today, in 1917.

26 English playwright William Shakespeare was baptized on this day, in 1564. (He was probably born 3 days earlier, but no one knows for sure.)

27 Today is *Freedom Day* in South Africa. It celebrates the day in 1994 when people of all races were allowed to vote in a general election for the first time.

28 The world's first space tourist, Dennis Tito, blasted off to the International Space Station in 2001. He paid Russia $20 million for the eight-day stay.

29 Britain's Prince William married Kate Middleton at Westminster Abbey in London in 2011. Two billion people watched on TV.

30 George Washington became the first President of the United States of America, in 1789.

BIRTHDAY CHALLENGE CHOOSER

Are you brave enough to let chance pick a challenge for you? If you're a fun-loving, adventurous ARIES, the answer is almost certainly "yes!" Make this Birthday Challenge Chooser for your own birthday, or for a friend's.

HOW TO MAKE IT:

1. Take an A4 piece of paper, and fold the bottom two corners up.

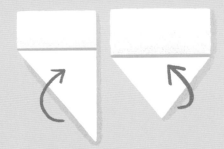

2. Cut off the top section of paper.

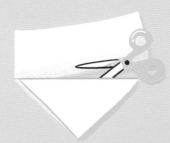
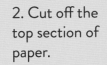

3. Unfold the paper. You should have a square piece of paper with an X crease.

4. Fold all four corners into the center.

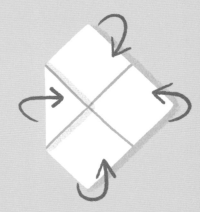

5. Flip the paper over.

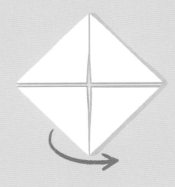

6. Fold all of the corners into the center again.

7. Number each flap, from 1 to 8.

46

8. Open up each flap and write an instruction inside—one for each number. You can use the ideas below, or make up your own.

Get across the room without touching the floor.

Get a friend to style your hair - blindfolded!

Walk 30 feet with a cup of water balanced on your head. (Make sure it's a plastic cup!)

For a certain time (1 minute for every year of your age), you're not allowed to say yes or no.

Unwrap a present using only your feet.

Challenge a friend: who can eat a whole slice of lemon first?

Slip something into someone's pocket without them noticing.

Tie your shoelace using just one hand.

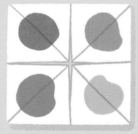

9. Flip the Birthday Challenge Chooser over and color in the four squares.

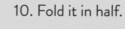

10. Fold it in half.

11. Insert your fingers inside the flaps to open it up.

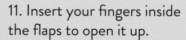

HOW YOU PLAY:

First pick a color. Spell out the color's name, opening and closing the Birthday Challenge Chooser once for each letter.

Then pick one of the numbers that you can see. Count to that number, opening and closing the Birthday Challenge Chooser as you go. Pick another number, and this time open up that flap and read the instruction inside.

What challenge has the Birthday Challenge Chooser set you? Remember, once a challenge has been chosen, there's no backing out!

01

Today is May Day, an ancient festival that celebrates the start of spring. The celebration traditionally involves dancing around maypoles.

MAY

What was happening in the world on the day you were born? Let's find out.

Emerald
BIRTHSTONE

Lily of the Valley and Hawthorn
BIRTH FLOWERS

(April 20–May 20)
TAURUS

(May 21–June 21)
GEMINI

01 see opposite page

02 You share your birthday with English soccer player David Beckham and American actor The Rock.

03 On this day in 1979, Margaret Thatcher was elected Prime Minister of Britain—the first woman to hold the post.

04 Today is *Star Wars Day*—May the Fourth be with you!

05 You share your birthday with English singer Adele.

06 The final episode of the TV series *FRIENDS* was shown today. It was watched by over 50 million people.

07 You share your birthday with Russian composer Tchaikovsky, who wrote the music for the ballets *Swan Lake* and *The Nutcracker*.

08 Today is *VE Day*, which marks the end of World War II in Europe in 1945. It's also the birthday of naturalist Sir David Attenborough.

09 You share your birthday with German student and heroine Sophie Scholl, who stood up to the Nazis. She was executed in 1943, at the age of 21.

10 In 1994, Nelson Mandela became South Africa's first black president.

11 The world's earliest surviving printed book, the Diamond Sūtra, dates back to this day in 868.

12 You share your birthday with Florence Nightingale, who looked after wounded soldiers in the Crimean War.

13 The world record for the highest standing jump on one leg was broken today, in 2017 Canadian Evan Ungar jumped on to a box over 4 feet high.

14 In 1973, the first space station, Skylab, was launched.

15 Today is *International Day of Families*. How nice! Birthdays are all about being with family and friends.

16 Today in 1975, Junko Tabei from Japan became the first woman to climb Mount Everest.

17 Today in 2009, Minecraft was released. It's the best-selling video game of all time.

18 You share your birthday with *International Museum Day*.

19 On this day in 2018, American actress Meghan Markle married Britain's Prince Harry at Windsor Castle.

20 Today is *World Bee Day*.

21 The first tweet was sent today in 2006, by Twitter co-founder Jack Dorsey.

22 The video game PacMan was released today in 1980.

23 Today is *World Turtle Day*—a day to celebrate and help protect turtles and tortoises around the world.

24 The first Eurovision Song Contest took place today in 1956. Switzerland won.

25 In a galaxy far, far away...Today in 1977, the first *Star Wars* film came out.

26 *Dracula* by Bram Stoker was published today in 1897.

27 Today in 1937, the Golden Gate Bridge in San Francisco was opened.

28 You share your birthday with Australian pop princess Kylie Minogue and *James Bond* author Ian Fleming.

29 In 1953, Tenzing Norgay and Edmund Hillary became the first to reach the summit of Everest, the world's tallest mountain.

30 Today in 1964, The Beatles' "Love Me Do" single went to Number 1 in the US.

31 You share your birthday with American poet Walt Whitman.

CREATIVE CARDS

If you need some inspiration, check out these ideas.

A home-made birthday card is the best sort of birthday card, especially if you're a talented TAURUS with oodles of creative flair at your fingertips.

Cut-up lots of old photographs of the person and arrange them to make a collage.

Draw a picture of a cake and glue a real birthday candle to the top of it.

Draw a picture of the person's star sign (see page 10) or Chinese horoscope animal (see page 14), and make up a funny horoscope prediction for the year ahead to go inside!

Glue colorful buttons or paper-covered candy onto a card and draw strings underneath them, to create a bunch of birthday balloons.

Decorate a card with dried flowers, using the person's favorite flower or birth month flower (see page 22). If you don't have a flower press, lay out the flowers between sheets of tissue paper, place inside the fold of a newspaper, and put a few heavy books on top. Flowers take 2-4 weeks to dry, so you will need to start early to get the card ready in time.

Create a birthday bunting card. To make the flags, cut diamond shapes from colorful paper or scraps of old material. Fold the diamonds in half and glue them down onto a short length of wool or string. Attach the bunting to the inside of the card, using sticky tape on the ends.

MAKE A POP-UP CARD

This sweet pop-up card, featuring a pile of presents, couldn't be simpler to make.

YOU NEED:

- 1 sheet of white card, trimmed so that it is slightly smaller than A4
- 1 sheet of colored A4 card
- Scissors
- To decorate—patterned paper, old magazines, scraps of material, ribbon
- Glue
- Coloring pens

HOW TO MAKE IT:

1. Fold a sheet of white card in half. From the folded edge, draw six lines, as shown here: 2 long lines (around 2 in.); 2 medium lines (around 1½ in.); and 2 short lines (around ¾ in.). Cut along each of the lines, then make creases at the ends of the cuts.

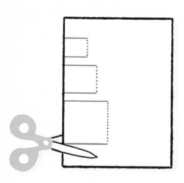

2. Fold open the card and "reverse" the creases, so that they point the other way. These are your "presents."

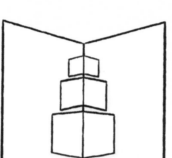

3. Cut out shapes the same size as your presents from patterned paper, magazines or material. Glue them on. Add small strips of ribbon to the sides of your presents.

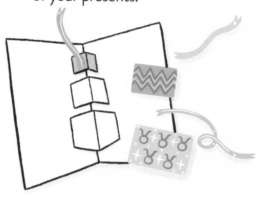

4. Now take the colored A4 sheet of card, and fold it in half. Glue your pop-out card onto the inside of the folded colored card, sticking it down one side at a time. Then add some final decorative touches!

TIP You can easily turn your pile of presents into a birthday cake—just add candles instead of ribbons!

FAN-TASTIC GARLANDS

Birthdays need color, and lots of it! No problem for creative TAUREANS— these color-popping home-made garlands are the perfect party decoration. In fact, they're so lovely you might want to leave them up all year round!

YOU NEED:

- A4 paper in lots of bright colors
- Glue stick
- 2 short lengths of string
- Stapler

1. Fold the A4 paper in half lengthways, and cut along the fold so that you have two long strips.

2. Take one of the strips of paper. Starting at one end, fold the paper backwards and forwards in a concertina fold. Each fold should be about 1 in. wide.

The big fans are made from a sheet of A4 paper, concertina-folded lengthways and stapled at the top.

This garland uses two different sized fans.

3. Fold the concertina paper in half, and stick the two halves together to create a mini fan.

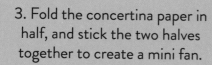

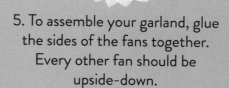

4. Repeat steps 1 to 3 to create lots of mini fans in lots of different colors.

5. To assemble your garland, glue the sides of the fans together. Every other fan should be upside-down.

6. When your garland is finished, staple a short length of string to either end, and hang it up where everyone can admire it!

Your mini fans can also be used to make a different style garland. Instead of sticking the fans to each other in step 5, attach them to a length of ribbon using a stapler.

The little fans are made from ¼ sheet of A4 paper.

JUNE

What was happening in the world on the day you were born? Let's find out.

Pearl
BIRTHSTONE

Rose and Honeysuckle
BIRTH FLOWER

(May 21–June 21)
GEMINI

(June 22–July 22)
CANCER

01 You share your birthday with iconic American actress Marilyn Monroe.

02 Today in 1953, Britain's Queen Elizabeth II was crowned in Westminster Abbey.

03 Today in 2017, Alex Honnold climbed the 3,600-foot-high El Capitan rock face in Yosemite National Park, USA—with no ropes!!! (see opposite page).

04 The first Pulitzer Prize was awarded today in 1917. It is given to outstanding journalists.

05 Today is **World Environment Day**, which encourages everyone to look after our amazing planet.

06 In 1984, the video game Tetris came out.

07 You share your birthday with American pop legend Prince and British TV survival expert Bear Grylls.

08 George Orwell's dystopian novel *Nineteen Eighty-Four* was published in 1949.

09 You share your birthday with American actors Natalie Portman and Michael J. Fox.

10 You share your birthday with Judy Garland, who starred as Dorothy in *The Wizard of Oz*.

11 The 1993 film *Jurassic Park* was released in the US today.

12 Today is **Anne Frank Day**. It celebrates the famous young diarist who went into hiding in Nazi-occupied Amsterdam in World War Two.

13 You share your birthday with Irish poet W. B. Yeats.

14 You share your birthday with Judith Kerr, author and illustrator of *The Tiger Who Came to Tea* picture book.

15 You share your birthday with actress Courtney Cox, who played Monica in the TV series *FRIENDS*.

16 In 1963, Russian cosmonaut Valentina Tereshkova became the first woman in space.

17 You share your birthday with American tennis ace Venus Williams.

18 You share your birthday with The Beatles star Paul McCartney.

19 In 2019, Kavitha M of India set a world record for the longest-held tree pose in yoga—55 minutes. Can you do better?

20 The classic film *Jaws* was released today in 1975.

21 Strike a (yoga) pose! Today is **International Day of Yoga**.

22 In 2015, Italian Silvio Sabba set a new record for the most coins stacked into a tower in a minute—69. How many can you manage?

23 The 1955 Disney film *Lady and the Tramp* was released today.

24 The longest tennis match ever played ended today in 2010, when John Isner beat Nicolas Mahut after 11 hours, 5 minutes of play over 3 days.

25 In 1678, Elena Cornaro Piscopia from Venice, Italy, became the first woman in the world to get a university doctoral degree (PhD).

26 J. K. Rowling's *Harry Potter and the Sorcerer's Stone* was published today in 1997.

27 In 1999, Tony Hawk became the first skateboarder to perform the difficult "900" trick—two-and-a-half spins in the air—and land it successfully.

28 The saxophone was patented today in 1846. It was named after its creator, musician Adolphe Sax.

29 Apple released the first iPhone today in 2007.

30 You share your birthday with speedy American swimmer Michael Phelps.

PARTY PLANNER QUIZ

Friendly GEMINIS love parties, but what sort of a party should you have? This fun quiz will help you (and your friends) decide. Just answer the questions and follow the arrows!

DO

BIKE

A day at a water park, or a day at the beach?

WATER PARK

Watch sport or do sport?

BEACH

Make a bug hotel, or make bath bombs?

BUG HOTEL

START HERE!
Would you rather...?

Go on a bike ride, or curl up with a book?

CAKE

BATH BOMBS

FILM

BOOK

Bake a cake, or make popcorn?

POPCORN

Chat to your friends, or watch *FRIENDS* on TV?

WATCHING FRIENDS

WATCH

ROCK CLIMBING

Go rock climbing or go rock pooling?

ROCK POOLING

On a rainy afternoon, watch a film, or do some art?

ART

CHAT

SLEEPING BAGS

Sociable sleeping bags, or your own snuggly bed all to yourself?

OWN BED

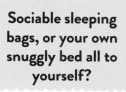

SPORTY PARTY
You are FULL of energy and love to be active. You need a party that puffs you out! How about roller-skating, swimming, climbing, or playing softball, soccer, or capture the flag in the local park?

NATURE PARTY
You love nature and being outdoors. Why not have a summer picnic party, or a camp out in the garden under the stars? If you're a winter baby, you can bring nature indoors instead—collect pebbles from the beach, for example, and paint them with your friends.

CREATIVE PARTY
Making things makes you happy. So roll up your sleeves and get creative with your friends. Choose your favorite activity—whether that's sculpting with clay or making fancy cookies—and design your party around it.

SLEEPOVER PARTY
The more time you can spend with your friends the better, as far as you're concerned! So invite your best pals round, pop on your PJs, plan your midnight feast, and stay up as late as you can get away with.

FILM NIGHT PARTY
You love your cosy creature comforts. For your perfect party, all you need is a fab film, a comfy couch, unlimited pizza, popcorn and ice-cream sundaes, and your best chums to share it all with.

BIG PARTY, SMALL PARTY?

This quiz will help you decide how big—or small—your party should be.
Use it to plan your own party, or to help friends plan theirs.

1. AT SCHOOL, HOW BIG IS YOUR GROUP OF FRIENDS?

A I've got a small group of close friends.
B I have one best friend, and they're amazing.
C I don't really have a group—I'm friends with everyone!

2. IT'S A WEAR-WHAT-YOU-LIKE DAY AT SCHOOL. WHAT DO YOU WEAR?

A The craziest outfit I can, of course—I want everyone to notice me!
B Probably just my favorite top and jeans. I don't want to stand out.
C My friends and I are going to co-ordinate our outfits, so we all look the same!

3. YOU'VE BEEN INVITED TO A PARTY BUT WILL ONLY KNOW A COUPLE OF PEOPLE THERE. HOW DO YOU FEEL?

A A bit nervous and shy.
B Sooooo excited! I love parties!
C So long as I know someone, I'll have a nice time.

4. YOU'RE STARTING AT A BRAND-NEW SCHOOL AND DON'T KNOW ANYONE. HOW DO YOU FEEL ON YOUR FIRST DAY?

A Excited. Think of all the new friends I can make—I might even have a new best friend by the end of the day!
B A bit shy. I hope I make some nice new friends.
C This is the worst day of my life. Ever.

5. AT SCHOOL, HOW WOULD YOU RATHER SPEND YOUR BREAKTIME?

A Chatting with a couple of friends.
B Reading a brilliant, page-turner book.
C Mucking about with a big gang of friends.

6. YOU'RE HAVING A SLEEPOVER. WHERE WOULD YOU LIKE IT TO BE?

A At my house, with my best friend.
B At a friend's house, with a few other friends—we can go a bit crazy and stay up late!
C On an overnight adventure camp, with loads of other kids.

7. YOUR SCHOOL IS HAVING A DANCE. WHAT'S YOUR FIRST REACTION?

A Are my friends going? If they are, I will.
B You must be kidding—there's no way you're making me go to that.
C Awesome! When is it? I need to practice my dance moves.

SCORING

Add up your scores, and then read on to find out what your total score means.

1. A=2, B=3, C=1
2. A=1, B=3, C=2
3. A=3, B=1, C=2
4. A=1, B=2, C=3
5. A=2, B=3, C=1
6. A=3, B=2, C=1
7. A=2, B=3, C=1

10 AND UNDER: You are the life and soul of the party. You love being around people, and they love being around you. How many people should you invite to your party? As many as you're allowed! The more people there are to celebrate with you, the happier you will be.

11–17: You like to be with your group of best friends—so long as they're at your party, you'll be happy. Just like Goldilocks, a massive party would be too big, and a tiny party too small, but a middle-sized party would be just about right!

18 AND OVER: You're happiest around the people you know best. A huge party with loads of people you don't know very well would be no fun at all, so keep your guest list small and ultra-exclusive!

24

The "lost" Inca city of Machu Picchu in Peru was rediscovered in 1911 by American archaeologist Hiram Bingham. Maybe one day you will visit it!

JULY

What was happening in the world on the day you were born? Let's find out.

Ruby
BIRTHSTONE

Larkspur and waterlily
BIRTH FLOWERS

June 22–July 22
CANCER

July 23–Aug 22
LEO

01 The very first Tour de France bicycle race pedaled off today in 1903.

02 Today in 2002, the first solo around-the-world balloon flight landed safely. It was American Steve Fossett's 6th attempt!

03 You share your birthday with American movie star Tom Cruise and German Formula 1 driver Sebastian Vettel.

04 Lewis Carroll's classic children's book, *Alice in Wonderland*, was published today in 1865.

05 In 1996 the first cloned mammal, Dolly the Sheep, was born. She was an identical copy of her mother.

06 You share your birthday with Mexican artist Frida Kahlo.

07 For lots of countries around the world, today is *World Chocolate Day*—yum!

08 In 1996, British girl band The Spice Girls released their first single, "Wannabe"—a song about Girl Power!

09 Nintendo character Mario made his first ever appearance in 1981, when the game Donkey Kong was released.

10 Earth's highest-ever temperature was recorded today in 1913, in Death Valley in the USA. It reached 134 °F. Phew!

11 Harper Lee's classic novel *To Kill a Mockingbird* was published today, in 1960.

12 You share your birthday with Malala Yousafzai, the Pakistani campaigner for girls' education. She won the Nobel Peace Prize aged just 17.

13 The first ever World Cup soccer matches kicked off today in Uruguay, in 1930. The hosts went on to win.

14 The first close-up photos of Mars were taken today in 1965, when the *Mariner 4* spacecraft flew past the planet.

15 In 1799, the Rosetta Stone was discovered, allowing experts to read Egyptian hieroglyphs for the first time.

16 Kissing was banned today, in 1439! England's King Henry VI announced the ban to try to stop the spread of the Black Death plague.

17 Today is *World Emoji Day*!

18 Today is *Nelson Mandela Day*, in honor of the South African politician and Nobel Prize winner, who was born on this day in 1918.

19 In 1545, the Tudor warship *Mary Rose* sank off the coast of England. It was raised from the sea over 400 years later, in 1982.

20 Today, in 1969, US astronaut Neil Armstrong became the first person to set foot on the Moon.

21 Earth's lowest-ever temperature was recorded today in 1983, in Antarctica. It was −128 °F. Brr!!!!

22 William Spooner was born today. He gave his name to "spoonerisms"—slips of the tongue where the letters of two words get mixed up. Bappy Hirthday!

23 Pop boy band One Direction was formed today during Britain's *X Factor* TV show.

24 see opposite page

25 In 1984, Russian cosmonaut Svetlana Savitskaya became the first woman to perform a space walk.

26 In 1983, Jarmila Kratochvílová from Czechoslovakia broke the women's 800-meter world record, in a time of 1 minute 53.28 seconds.

27 In 1993, Javier Sotomayor from Cuba jumped 8.03 feet in the high jump, setting a new men's world record.

28 Beatrix Potter, English author of *The Tale of Peter Rabbit*, was born today in 1866.

29 NASA was created today, in 1958.

30 Today is the *International Day of Friendship*. What a nice day to have a birthday!

31 You share your birthday with *Harry Potter* author, J.K. Rowling.

SECRET NOTE AMBUSH

If you want to really make your grown-up happy on their birthday, set up a Secret Note Ambush. First, write lots of little notes listing all the things you love about them (grown-ups are very soppy and will love this), and then smuggle the notes into lots of different places for your grown-up to find throughout the day—in their slippers, in a coat pocket, wrapped around the toothpaste tube, at the bottom of their favorite mug, in their handbag, in the fridge, on the car windscreen. You could even unwind a bit of the toilet paper and write them a note on that.

HEAD OF THE TABLE

In Israel, the birthday child gets to sit in a specially decorated chair and wear a garland on their head. You can copy this idea and decorate a chair for your grown-up to sit in while they have their birthday breakfast or dinner. Tie on balloons, streamers, or fresh flowers, and make them a birthday crown to match.

GROWN-UP BIRTHDAYS

Grown-up birthdays just aren't as much fun as kids' birthdays. Sad, isn't it? Poor grown-ups. But fortunately, kind, family-loving CANCERIANS are on hand to help. Here are some ideas on how to make your grown-up's birthday more fun by being extra-specially nice to them.

BALLOON ATTACK

Set up a surprise Birthday Balloon Attack for your grown-up. Fill their closet, or a large kitchen cabinet, or any other small area in the house with balloons—when they open the door, the balloons will rush out and surprise them. To make the balloon attack even more fun, hide a secret message in one of the balloons before you blow it up—maybe this could be a clue leading your grown-up to their birthday card or present. When the balloons are all blown up, write "Pop me!" on the balloon with the message inside, and happy birthday messages on all of the others. Your grown-up will need to find the special balloon to discover the secret message.

BIRTHDAY COUNTDOWN

Make your grown-up a Paperchain Birthday Countdown, to count down the days until their birthday. Every day they can remove one link of the paperchain.

It's up to you how long you make the paperchain. To make a paperchain for a week's countdown, cut seven strips of colorful paper. On one side of the strips, write the numbers 1 to 7. On the other side, write down something that will make your grown-up cheerful on each of the seven days of the countdown—this could be a CLUE about where you have hidden a small chocolate or other gift, a PROMISE from you to do a chore or give them a hug, or a CHALLENGE that they have to complete that day (2 days to go? maybe they have to endure a 2-minute cold shower).

When your strips are finished, assemble your paperchain one loop at a time, and hang it up with the number 1 at the top.

07

In 1974, daredevil Philippe Petit walked across a tightrope between two skyscrapers in New York City—with no safety net!

AUGUST

What was happening in the world on the day you were born? Let's find out.

Peridot
BIRTHSTONE

Gladiolus and Poppy
BIRTH FLOWERS

(July 23–Aug 22)
LEO

(Aug 23–Sept 22)
VIRGO

01 You share your birthday with intrepid explorer William Clark, who led the famous Lewis and Clark Expedition across uncharted America in the early 19th century.

02 Today in 2018 Masud Rana from Bangladesh set a new world record by swimming 50 meters in 44.95 seconds with a soccer ball balanced on his head!

03 You share your birthday with Creme Puff, the oldest cat ever. She lived for an incredible 38 years and 3 days!

04 You share your birthday with former American President Barack Obama, and jazz legend Louis Armstrong.

05 You share your birthday with Neil Armstrong, the first person to walk on the Moon.

06 The world's first website went online today in 1991. It was created by Tim Berners-Lee.

07 see opposite page

 08 Today is *International Cat Day*—so if you have a cat, give it a cuddle!

09 In 1483, the Sistine Chapel opened in the Vatican, in Rome, Italy. It is famous for its ceiling paintings by Michelangelo.

10 The Louvre art museum opened in Paris today, in 1793.

11 Today is *Mountain Day* in Japan—a day to celebrate (you guessed it!) mountains.

12 One of Mars's two moons, Deimos, was discovered today in 1877 by astronomer Asaph Hall. Phobos, the other moon, was found six days later.

13 American swimmer Michael Phelps won his 23rd Olympic gold medal at the 2016 Rio Olympics, making him the most decorated Olympian of all time.

14 The first Youth Olympics—for athletes aged 15 to 18—kicked off today in 2010, in Singapore.

15 You share your birthday with *Hunger Games* actress Jennifer Lawrence.

16 In 2009, Usain Bolt from Jamaica ran the 100 meters in 9.58 seconds, winning an Olympic gold and becoming the fastest person ever.

17 George Orwell's famous novel, *Animal Farm*, was published today in 1946.

18 In 1983, 12-year-old Samantha Druce swam the English Channel between France and Britain—the youngest female ever to do it.

19 You share your birthday with Coco Chanel, the French fashion designer who founded the Chanel company.

20 In 1977, the *Voyager 2* space probe was launched. It reached Jupiter in 1979, Saturn in 1981 and Uranus in 1986, and is still going!

21 The Disney animated film *Bambi* was released today in 1942.

22 The world record for the highest jump by a pig was set today in 2004, when Kotetsu, a pot-bellied pig from Japan, jumped 2 feet and 3 inches.

23 The hashtag was first used in a tweet today in 2007. #cool!

24 In 79 CE, Mount Vesuvius erupted, burying the ancient Roman town of Pompeii. You can visit the excavated town today.

25 Today in 2018, Saori Yoshida from Japan set a new world record for the most balloons burst by sitting on them in 1 minute. She managed 123!

26 The Beatles' song "Hey Jude" was released today in 1968.

27 The 1964 musical *Mary Poppins* was released today.

28 In 1963, American civil rights activist Martin Luther King Jr made his famous "I have a dream" speech, calling for an end to racism.

29 In 2008, 14-year-old Hou Yifan from China became the youngest female Grandmaster—a title given to the world's best chess players.

30 You share your birthday with 19th-century English novelist Mary Shelley, who wrote *Frankenstein*.

31 The world record for the most press-ups in an hour was broken in 2018 by Australian Jarrad Young. He managed 2,806—around 47 a minute!

MAGIC MIXOLOGY

There are two mocktail recipes to get you started on the opposite page. But the best thing about making mocktails is coming up with your own crazy combinations! Here are some ideas.

To make a fresh strawberry syrup (enough for 6 mocktails), chop up 10.5 oz of strawberries and gently heat them in a pan with 3.5 oz of sugar and 1 tbsp of lemon juice. Simmer for around 15 minutes until the syrup has reduced by a third, then leave to cool. Blend when cool. **Take care when heating the syrup, as it can get very hot. Always ask an adult for help and advice.**

START WITH...

FRUIT JUICE
apple, orange, cranberry, pineapple

FRESHLY SQUEEZED LIME AND LEMON JUICE

FIZZY SODA
lemonade, soda water, ginger beer

FRUIT SYRUP
you can buy grenadine or make your own fruit syrup

ICE   Freeze ingredients into your ice for extra fun!

BERRIES

MINT

EDIBLE FLOWERS

Make **STRIPY ICE CUBES** by freezing fruit juice in layers

FINAL TOUCHES...

Add a swizzle stick—thread it with fruit or gummi bears

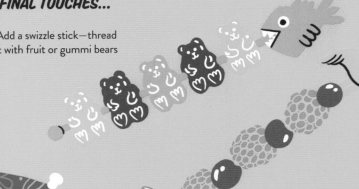

Add an umbrella and paper straw

Don't forget to name your creation!

Before the party, coat the rims of your mocktail glasses with sugar sprinkles, edible glitter, or freeze-dried fruit sprinkles. To make the sprinkles stick, dip the rim of the glass first into water, then into the sprinkles. You can also dip the rims of the glasses into melted chocolate, let it cool slightly and then sprinkle with popping candy and leave to set.

RAINBOW COOLER

1. Coat the rim of your glass with freeze-dried raspberries.

2. Pour a layer of fruit syrup into the glass.

3. Add a fruit swizzle stick, and then fill the glass with lots of ice cubes (this makes it easier to form the other layers).

4. Pour some orange juice VERY SLOWLY into the glass. It should form a separate layer. Allow the layers to settle.

5. Add a drop of blue food coloring to some soda water, and pour it VERY SLOWLY into the glass to form a new layer.

6. Serve with a colorful cocktail umbrella, and enjoy!

When you're making layered mocktails, remember that more sugary liquids (like syrups) will sink to the bottom.

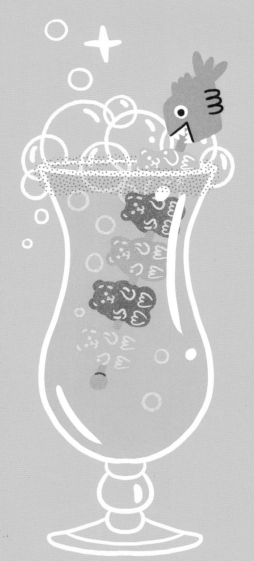

PINK POPPING FIZZER

1. Coat the rim of your glass with edible glitter.

2. Pour a layer of fruit syrup into the glass, add cranberry juice and 2 tbsp of lemon juice, and stir.

3. Add a couple of ice cubes, and a gummi bear swizzle stick.

4. Working quickly, pour in a teaspoon of popping candy and ¼ teaspoon of baking soda, and stir vigorously with the swizzle stick. Your fizzing, frothing creation is now ready to drink!

SEPTEMBER

What was happening in the world on the day you were born? Let's find out.

Sapphire
BIRTHSTONE

Aster and Morning Glory
BIRTH FLOWERS

(Aug 23–Sept 22)
VIRGO

(Sept 23–Oct 23)
LIBRA

01 World War II started today in 1939. It ended six years and one day later.

02 In 1666, the Great Fire of London broke out. In four days, it destroyed a third of the city.

03 The online auction website eBay was founded today in 1995.

04 The company Google was founded today in 1998.

05 In 1977, the *Voyager 1* space probe was launched. It's now left the solar system, and is still in touch with Earth!

06 In 1522, Ferdinand Magellan's ship *Victoria* became the first to circumnavigate the world.

07 You share your birthday with Elizabeth I, Queen of England from 1559 to 1603.

08 The first episode of the TV series *Star Trek* was shown today in 1966.

09 You share your birthday with the great Russian novelist Leo Tolstoy.

10 In 2008, the largest machine in the world was switched on—CERN's Large Hadron Collider, in Switzerland.

11 Enid Blyton's *Five on a Treasure Island* (the first "Famous Five" book) was published in 1942.

12 In 1940, the famous Lascaux prehistoric cave paintings were discovered in France.

13 You share your birthday with Roald Dahl, author of *Matilda* and *Charlie and the Chocolate Factory*.

14 The dystopian novel *The Hunger Games*, by Suzanne Collins, was published today in 2008.

15 You share your birthday with novelist Agatha Christie, creator of fictional detectives Hercule Poirot and Miss Marple.

16 You share your birthday with American blues musician B. B. King, and Julia Donaldson, author of *The Gruffalo*.

17 William Golding's *Lord of the Flies* was published today in 1954.

18 In 2014, Ahmed Gabr scuba dived to a depth of 1,090 feet in the Red Sea, Egypt—the deepest-ever dive.

19 On this day in 1783, a duck, a rooster and a sheep called Montauciel became the first living creatures to fly in a balloon (see opposite page).

20 In 1973, Billie Jean King played Bobby Riggs in the famous "battle of the sexes" tennis match. Riggs bet that he could beat any female player—and lost!

21 J. R. R. Tolkien's *The Hobbit* was published today in 1937.

22 Today is **World Rhino Day**—a day to celebrate and help protect these beautiful beasts.

23 The video games company Nintendo was founded today, in 1889. Back then, it sold playing cards.

24 Elvis Presley released the song "Jailhouse Rock" today in 1957.

25 Your share your birthday with American actors Mark Hamill (Luke Skywalker in *Star Wars*) and Will Smith.

26 You share your birthday with American tennis star Serena Williams and poet T. S. Eliot.

27 The discovery of a completely new species was confirmed today in 2017—a giant tree rat known as "vika"!

28 Chinese philosopher Confucius was born today in 551 BCE. He said, "Our greatest glory is not in never falling, but in rising every time we fall."

29 The world record for the women's 200 meters (21.34 seconds) was set in 1988 by Florence Griffith-Joyner.

30 You share your birthday with Max Verstappen, the youngest driver to win a Formula One World Championship race (aged 18).

HOME-MADE HEART COOKIES

VIRGOS love to be kind, and what better way is there to show someone how much you care than by whipping up a batch of yummy heart-shaped cookies for their birthday?

YOU NEED:

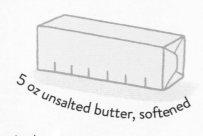
5 oz unsalted butter, softened

3.5 oz sugar

a pinch of salt

1 tsp vanilla extract

1 egg

boiled sweets in different colors

1 tsp baking powder

9 oz plain flour plus a bit

extra for flouring the work surface

HOW TO MAKE THEM:

01

Preheat the oven to 350 °F (180 °C/Gas 4) and line a baking tray with baking paper. Using an electric mixer, mix together the butter and sugar in a large bowl until it is pale and fluffy. Beat in the egg.

02

Sieve the flour, baking powder and salt into the bowl. Add the vanilla extract and mix with a wooden spoon to form a soft cookie dough.

03

Flour the work surface, then roll out your dough until it is about ½ in. thick. Use a heart-shaped cutter to cut out heart shapes. If you don't have a cutter, you can make a heart-shaped template from paper instead—place the template on the dough and carefully cut around it using a small knife. Once you have cut out the cookies, move them onto the baking tray, leaving about ¾ in. between each one.

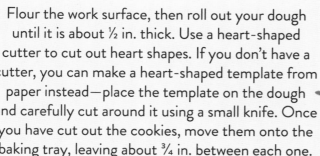

04

Use a smaller cutter or a small knife to cut out a heart shape in the center of each cookie.

05

Separate your boiled sweets into different colors and place them in separate sandwich bags. Press out the air, seal the bags, and then use a rolling pin to (gently) bash each bag to crush the sweets into small grains.

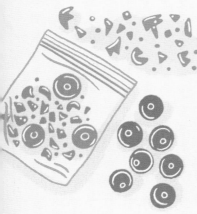

BE SENSIBLE AND TAKE CARE WHEN YOU ARE USING A HOT OVEN, SHARP KNIFE, OR ELECTRIC BEATERS. ALWAYS ASK AN ADULT FOR HELP AND ADVICE.

TIP
YOU CAN MAKE EACH COOKIE A DIFFERENT COLOR, OR MIX UP THE COLORS AND GO WILD!

06

Sprinkle the crushed sweets into the cookie holes, being careful not to overfill them.

07

Cook in the preheated oven until the cookies are golden and the sweets have melted—this should take about 15 minutes. Leave the biscuits to cool for 5 minutes on the tray before transferring them to a cooling rack.

08

Choose the wonkiest biscuit to taste-test. Are they a success, or do you need to taste another one to be absolutely, positively sure…?

31

If you live in North America or the UK, you can spend your birthday carving pumpkins and trick or treating—today is Halloween!

OCTOBER

What was happening in the world on the day you were born? Let's find out.

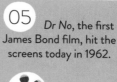
Opal
BIRTHSTONE

Marigold and Cosmos
BIRTH FLOWERS

(Sept 23–Oct 23)
LIBRA

(Oct 24–Nov 21)
SCORPIO

01 *Little Women* by Louisa May Alcott was published today in 1868. Have you read it?

02 You share your birthday with a bunny—Beatrix Potter's *The Tale of Peter Rabbit* was published in 1902.

03 The first women's official marathon record was recorded today, in 1926. Violet Piercy ran the 26-mile course in 3 hours and 40 minutes.

04 *Sputnik 1*, the first-ever satellite, was launched into space in 1957. It was the size of a beach ball.

05 *Dr No*, the first James Bond film, hit the screens today in 1962.

06 In 2007, Jason Lewis became the first person to circumnavigate the world using human power—walking, swimming, rowing, and cycling—and it took him 4,833 days.

07 Humans saw the far "dark" side of the Moon for the first time today, in 1959, when a space probe took a photo.

08 Wangari Maathai, an activist from Kenya, became the first African woman to win the Nobel Peace Prize, in 2004.

09 You share your birthday with John Lennon from The Beatles, and American anti-slavery activist Mary Ann Shadd Cary.

10 Today in 1967 the "Outer Space Treaty" came into being. It stated that space belonged to everyone.

11 Kathryn Dwyer Sullivan became the first American woman to walk in space today, in 1984.

12 Christopher Columbus got his first sighting of the "New World" (the Americas) today in 1492—though he thought it was Asia!

13 Happy Birthday Paddington Bear! The first book featuring the marmalade-loving bear from Peru was published today in 1958.

14 In 2012, Austrian skydiver Felix Baumgerter took a giant balloon up into space and then parachuted back to Earth! In freefall, he reached speeds of over 800 mph.

15 A French teacher became the first person to go up in a balloon today in 1783. (He wasn't the first living thing though—see September 19th.)

16 In 1986, mountaineer Reinhold Messner became the first person to climb all 14 of the world's highest peaks.

17 A chess game, called "the Game of the Century," was played today in 1956. Chess master Donald Byrne lost to 13-year-old, Bobby Fischer.

18 Walt Disney's *The Jungle Book* film was released today in 1967.

19 You share your birthday with Philip Pullman, author of *The Northern Lights* trilogy.

20 The Sydney Opera House was opened today in 1973.

21 You share your birthday with actress Carrie Fisher, who played Princess Leia in the *Star Wars* films.

22 The first parachute jump took place today in 1779. Frenchman André-Jacques Garnerin leapt out of a balloon using a hand-made silk parachute.

23 The Walt Disney film *Dumbo* came out today in 1941.

24 The world's very first soccer club, Sheffield FC, was founded in England today in 1857.

25 You share your birthday with the famous painter Pablo Picasso and the American singer Katy Perry.

26 On this day in 2017 Jacinda Ardern became prime minister of New Zealand at the age of 37—the world's youngest head of government.

27 Water skis were patented today in 1925. Maybe one day you'll try water skiing yourself!

28 Today is *International Animation Day*, celebrating the amazing art of animated films.

29 In 1998, 77-year-old American astronaut John Glenn became the oldest person to fly in space.

30 The world's most expensive cheesecake sold today, in 2017, for $4,592.42. Crazy!

31 see opposite page

LOOKING BACK

Look back at the year just gone and write a list of everything you've done since your last birthday that you're proud of. Have you:

• gained any new skills? Perhaps you've begun baking, got better at playing a musical instrument, or taught yourself how to juggle.

• done something scary? Maybe you've performed in a play, entered a race, or stood up to talk in front of your class when you *really* didn't want to.

• helped the planet? Have you picked up litter, walked or cycled more, or reminded your family to recycle?

• been kind or thoughtful to others, or gone out of your way to help someone?

Write down all of your achievements, big and small, and then give yourself a big pat on the back. Well done!

A birthday is the perfect time for reflecting on the year just gone and the year to come, especially for thoughtful, balanced LIBRANS.

BE GRATEFUL FOR RIGHT NOW

You might have heard that regularly thinking about things we feel grateful for can help us feel happier. It's true. Try it, right now: Think of three things that you are grateful for.

Now look forward to the year to come.

Write a letter to yourself, seal it and then ask your parent or grown-up to keep it and give it to you on your birthday next year. Here are some ideas for things you could include:

- the things you like doing best

- who your closest friends are

- anything you are looking forward to, or not looking forward to, in the coming year

- what makes you happy and what makes you sad

- what you are worried about

- a list of your hopes and ambitions for the year to come

- a prediction for the future. Pick one thing that you think will be different in the world when you read your letter in a year's time. Remember to wish yourself a happy birthday too!

In one year's time, open and read your letter and see how much you have (or haven't) changed. Did you manage to achieve any of your ambitions for the year? Now you can write a new letter for your next birthday.

They can be anything you like—a person, a thing, or something nice that happened to you today.

Practicing gratitude is a really good habit to develop. Why not try to do it at the end of every day, starting today?

NOVEMBER

What was happening in the world on the day you were born? Let's find out.

Topaz — BIRTH STONE

Chrysanthemum — BIRTH FLOWER

Oct 24–Nov 21 — SCORPIO

Nov 22 – Dec 21 — SAGITTARIUS

01 The Oscar-winning film *Titanic* was released today in 1997.

02 Today is **All Soul's Day**—the final day of Mexico's **Day of the Dead** celebrations (see opposite page).

03 Today in 1906, the Morse code signal "SOS" (· · · – – – · · ·) was recognized as the worldwide signal for "Help."

04 In 2019, a record was set for the most pencils balanced on the back of a hand in 30 seconds—41! How many can you manage?

05 Today is **Guy Fawkes Night** in the UK, celebrated with bonfires, fireworks and, in some towns, spectacular torchlit processions.

06 You share your birthday with American actress Emma Stone.

07 You share your birthday with Nobel-prize winning scientist Marie Curie.

08 Brazilian surfer Rodrigo Koxa broke the record for the biggest wave ever surfed in 2017. It was 80 feet high.

09 You share your birthday with Hollywood actress and inventor Hedy Lamarr, who was born in 1914.

10 Today is **World Science Day**. Maybe one day YOU will make a great scientific discovery!

11 World War 1 ended in 1918 on this day at 11am, "the eleventh hour of the eleventh day of the eleventh month."

12 In 2014, the space probe *Philae* became the first to land on a comet.

13 Today is **World Kindness Day**— what a lovely day to have a birthday!

14 You share your birthday with the great Impressionist painter Claude Monet.

15 You share your birthday with the American painter Georgia O'Keeffe, famous for her paintings of flowers.

16 The first *Harry Potter* film was released today, in 2001.

17 The record for the most ice-cream scoops balanced on a cone—125!—was recorded today in 2018.

18 You share your birthday with 19th-century women's and civil rights activist Sojourner Truth.

19 The world record for balancing on a bicycle was set today in 1982—Rudi Jan Jozef De Greef from Belgium managed 10 hours!

20 In 1998 the first module of the International Space Station was launched.

21 Today is **World Hello Day**! All you need to do to take part is say hello to at least 10 people.

22 In 1995, the first *Toy Story* film was released.

23 The first episode of the British TV sci-fi show *Doctor Who* aired today, in 1963.

24 In 1877, *Black Beauty* by Anna Sewell was published.

25 The first known koala twins were born today in 1999. Koala twins are super rare!

26 In 2013, a copy of the 17th-century *Bay Psalm Book* sold for $14,165,000—the most expensive book ever sold.

27 The Disney film *Frozen* came out today in 2013.

28 You share your birthday with English poet William Blake. One of his most famous poems is *The Tyger*.

29 You share your birthday with Louisa May Alcott, author of *Little Women*, and C. S. Lewis, author of the *Narnia* books.

30 Your share your birthday with British wartime prime minister Winston Churchill, famous for his inspiring speeches.

FORTUNE-TELLING CAKE

Hands up if you like the idea of having a magic fortune-telling cake on your birthday. Of course you do, especially if you're a mysterious SCORPIO—or maybe your psychic powers mean you know everyone's fortunes already.

Fortune-telling cakes have been around for ages. Traditionally, metal charms representing different fortunes were baked into the cake. When the cake was cut, some people would find a lucky charm in their slice—if they weren't unlucky enough to choke on it or break a tooth first.

To make your own, slightly less dangerous fortune-telling cake, all you need to do is tie some lucky charms (one for each guest) onto long, thin ribbons, and then hide the charms under the bottom of the cake. After the candles have been blown out, everyone chooses a ribbon and pulls out a charm to reveal their fortune. Good luck!

SHOOTING STAR
Your wish will be granted.

PALM TREE
Your life will be filled with travel.

OWL
You will lead a wise life.

ICE-CREAM CONE
Your life will be lots and lots of fun.

HOW TO MAKE THE CHARMS:

You can buy cake charms online, or you can make your own—shrink plastic is brilliant for this (but make sure, before you put it in the oven, that you have made a hole that will be big enough to thread a thin ribbon through once the plastic has shrunk). Instead of using charms, you could also write the fortunes onto small slips of paper, roll them up tightly and tie the ribbon around them. There are some ideas for charms and fortunes below.

LOVE HEART
You will be surrounded by love in your life.

HOT-AIR BALLOON
You will have a life of excitement and adventure.

TORTOISE
You will live a long and happy life.

FOUR-LEAF CLOVER
Good luck will find you.

DOG
Your life will be full of loyal friends.

14

In 1911, Norwegian explorer Roald Amundsen and four of his team became the first people to reach the South Pole.

DECEMBER

What was happening in the world on the day you were born? Let's find out.

Tanzanite
BIRTHSTONE

Narcissus, Holly, and Poinsetta
BIRTH FLOWERS

(Nov 22–Dec 21)
SAGITTARIUS

(Dec 22–Jan 19)
CAPRICORN

01 Today in 1955, in Montgomery, Alabama, Rosa Parks changed history when she refused to give up her seat on the bus to a white passenger.

02 The first pizza party in space was held today in 2017, by astronauts aboard the International Space Station.

03 In 2019, Álvaro Martín Mendieta set a record-breaking time for tying three pairs of shoelaces—11.32 seconds. Can you do better?

04 You share your birthday with Russian abstract painter Wassily Kandinsky and American rapper Jay-Z.

05 You share your birthday with American animator Walt Disney.

06 In 1912, archaeologists found the 3,300-year-old bust of the great Egyptian queen Nefertiti.

07 You share your birthday with Madame Tussaud, founder of the famous wax museum in London.

08 Today in 2019, Kim Surim from North Korea memorized 2,530 playing cards in an hour—a new world record!

09 You share your birthday with British actress Judy Dench.

10 The first Nobel Prizes were awarded today, in 1901.

11 You share your birthday with pioneering American astronomer Annie Jump Cannon.

12 You share your birthday with American crooner Frank Sinatra.

13 You share your birthday with American singer-songwriter Taylor Swift. She signed her first record deal aged 15.

14 see opposite page

15 In 1612, Andromeda—our closest galaxy—was seen through a telescope for the first time.

16 You share your birthday with author Jane Austen.

17 Today in 1903, the Wright brothers made the first powered airplane flight. It lasted 12 seconds.

18 You share your birthday with singer Billie Eilish, actor Brad Pitt, and film director Steven Spielberg.

19 In 1843, *A Christmas Carol* by Charles Dickens was published.

20 *Grimms' Fairy Tales* was published today in 1812.

21 The world's first ever website (info.cern.ch) went live today in 1990. It still exists—check it out!

22 The first ever X-ray was taken in 1895, by its inventor, Wilhelm Röntgen. He X-rayed his wife's hand.

23 In 2019, 16-year-old climate activist Greta Thunberg appeared on the cover of *Time* magazine as their youngest-ever "Person of the Year."

24 The Christmas Truce began today in 1914, in the World War 1 trenches. British and German soldiers sang carols and played soccer.

25 Happy Birthday Christmas babies! You share your birthday with the great scientist Isaac Newton.

26 You share your birthday with Charles Babbage, who invented the first mechanical computer in the 1830s.

27 You share your birthday with French scientist Louis Pasteur, who discovered vaccination.

28 Neptune was spotted for the first time today in 1612, by astronomer Galileo.

29 You share your birthday with former US president Andrew Johnson and former British prime minister William Gladstone.

30 You share your birthday with *Jungle Book* author Rudyard Kipling, and American golfer Tiger Woods.

31 Lucky you: you share your birthday with great Impressionist painter Henri Matisse, PLUS it's New Year's Eve, when everybody is in a party mood.

FELIZ CUMPLEAÑOS, BON AI

QUÉBÉCOIS
Bonne Fête
("Good party")

Quebec, Canada

GERMAN
Alles Gute zum Geburtstag
("All the best on your birthday")

ENGLISH
Happy Birthday

YORUBA
O ku ojo ibi
("Happy birthday")

PORTUGUESE
Feliz Aniversário
("Happy Anniversary")

Nigeria

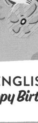

Brazil

THE BIRTHDAY SONG IN GERMAN

Zum Geburtstag viel Glück!
Zum Geburtstag viel Glück!
Zum Geburtstag liebe (person's name)
Zum Geburtstag viel Glück!

SPANISH
Feliz Cumpleaños
("Happy Completed Years")

THE BIRTHDAY SONG IN FRENCH

Joyeux anniversaire!
Joyeux anniversaire!
Joyeux anniversaire
(person's name)
Joyeux anniversaire!

THE BIRTHDAY SONG IN SPANISH

¡Cumpleaños feliz,
Cumpleaños feliz,
Te deseamos (person's name)
Cumpleaños feliz!

Argentina

...NIVERSAIRE, HAPPY BIRTHDAY!

If you're an adventurous **SAGITTARIUS**, you love to meet new people and explore the world. Let's find out how people in other countries wish their friends and family a happy birthday. How many different greetings can you learn? Think of all the new friends you could make someday.

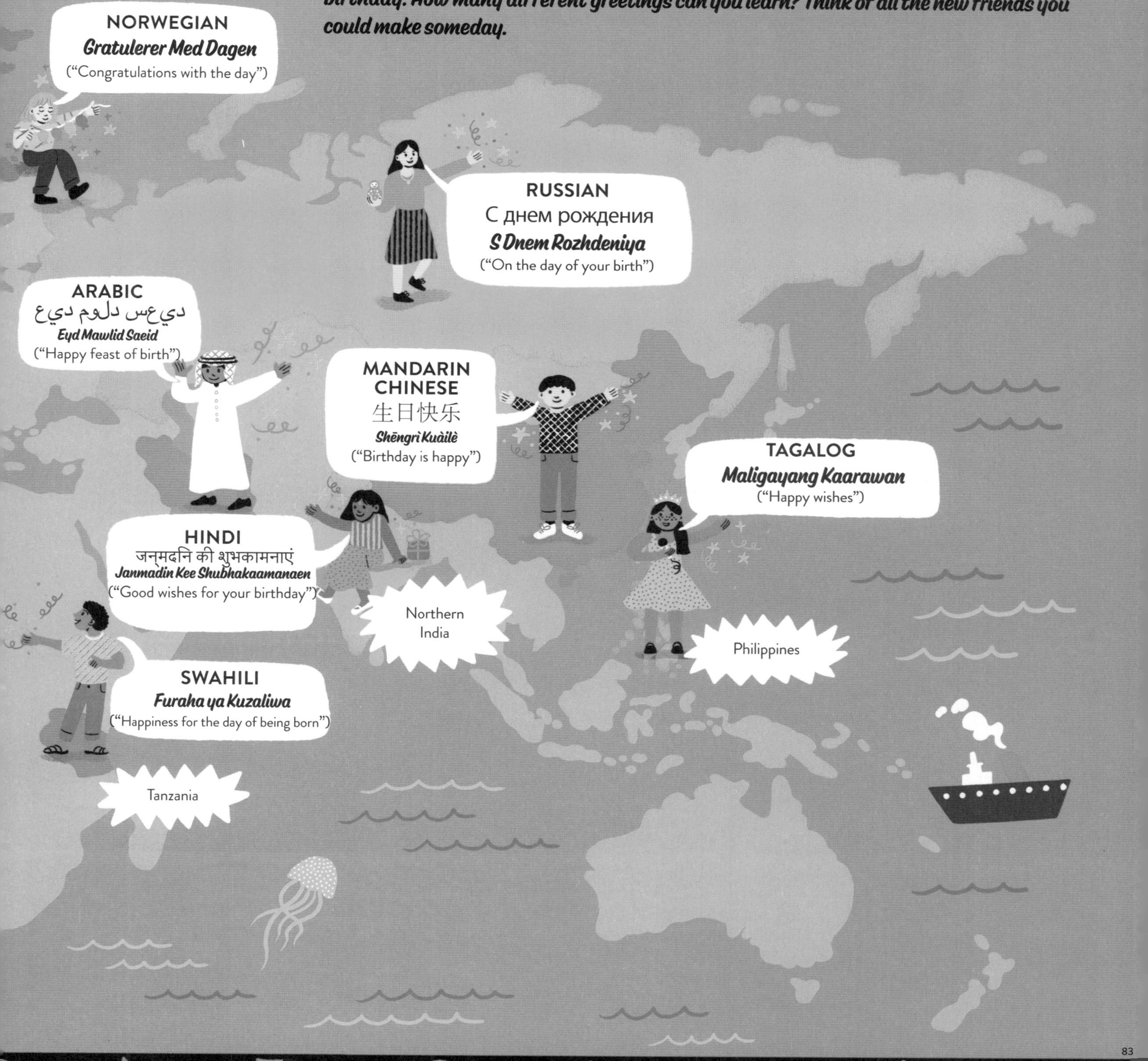

NORWEGIAN
Gratulerer Med Dagen
("Congratulations with the day")

RUSSIAN
С днем рождения
S Dnem Rozhdeniya
("On the day of your birth")

ARABIC
عيد مولد سعيد
Eyd Mawlid Saeid
("Happy feast of birth")

**MANDARIN
CHINESE**
生日快乐
Shēngrì Kuàilè
("Birthday is happy")

TAGALOG
Maligayang Kaarawan
("Happy wishes")

HINDI
जन्मदिन की शुभकामनाएं
Janmadin Kee Shubhakaamanaen
("Good wishes for your birthday")

Northern
India

Philippines

SWAHILI
Furaha ya Kuzaliwa
("Happiness for the day of being born")

Tanzania

CHAPTER 3

DID YOU KNOW?: BIRTHDAY TRIVIA

Do you know how many birthdays the Queen of England has each year? Or how much the world's most expensive birthday cake cost? (Have a guess!) Whereabouts in the world do you think you might you end up face-first in your own birthday cake? And which animal do you share your age with? Delve into this chapter to find the answers, and along the way discover lots more weird and wonderful facts about the very best day of the year!

BIRTHDAYS AROUND THE WORLD

How would you like to celebrate your birthday by being bumped on the ground, covered in flour or cinnamon, or made to tidy up lots of rubbish? These are just some of the bizarre birthday traditions that take place around the world.

In Mexico, blowing out the birthday candles can be a bit of a messy business. La mordida is a tradition which involves shoving the birthday child's face into the cake while everyone around them shouts "Mordida! Mordida! Mordida!" (or "Bite! Bite! Bite!") Hopefully the cake frosting is tasty.

In some parts of eastern Canada, children have to watch out for sneaky parents creeping up on them to smear their noses with butter. Nose greasing supposedly makes the person so slippery that bad luck can't catch hold of them.

Getting covered with masses of flour is a birthday tradition on the island of Jamaica, in the Caribbean. Sometimes the birthday boy or girl is splashed with water first, to make the flour extra-hard to wash off—now that's just mean!

There is a tradition in some parts of Germany that if a man is unmarried on his 30th birthday, he has to sweep up the rubbish on the steps of the town hall or local church. The man's friends "help" him by throwing rubbish on the steps. The idea is that any unmarried woman who happens to be passing will see how tidy and helpful he would be around the house.

In Denmark, unmarried 25-year-olds traditionally get covered head to foot with cinnamon on their birthday. Sometimes they are pelted with eggs first, to make sure the cinnamon sticks. Yuk! On their 30th birthday, the cinnamon is swapped for pepper.

Some birthday traditions involve being pulled, punched or bumped— ouch! In Argentina, birthdays are marked by ear lobe pulling, one pull for each year. Friendly birthday punches are sometimes given in some countries, including the US. And in Britain and Ireland, the tradition of the "birthday bumps" involves the child being picked up by their arms and legs and "bumped" on the floor, once for each year, plus one for luck.

HOW MANY SALS ARE YOU?

It's not just birthdays that can be very different around the globe—some parts of the world even measure age differently, too. In most countries, you turn one year old when you have been alive for exactly one year, but in South Korea many people still use a traditional system that measures age in units called "sals." A person is considered to be one sal (year) old on the day they are born, and they turn one sal (year) older not on their actual birthday, but on New Year's Day. This means that a baby who is born on the 31st December would turn two the following day. If you were measuring your age in sals, how old would you be?

SPECIAL BIRTHDAYS

All birthdays are special, but some birthdays are a little bit more special than others!

The Queen of England's birthday is so special she has two of them! Her real birthday is on April 21, but she also has an "official" birthday on a Saturday in June, which is celebrated with a parade called Trooping the Color. The royal "two birthdays" tradition began over 270 years ago when King George II decided to move his birthday parade from November (when his actual birthday was) to the summer, so that everyone could enjoy it in the sunshine.

In Judaism, a boy becomes a "bar mitzvah" on his 13th birthday, and a girl becomes "bat mitzvah" when she is 12. At these ages, children become adults in the Jewish community, so they are very important birthdays.

The quinceañera (which means "fifteen years" in Spanish) is a big celebration for a girl's 15th birthday that is celebrated in Mexico and other countries. The girl wears a beautiful ballgown to her party, and dances a waltz with her father. Everybody toasts her becoming a grown-up.

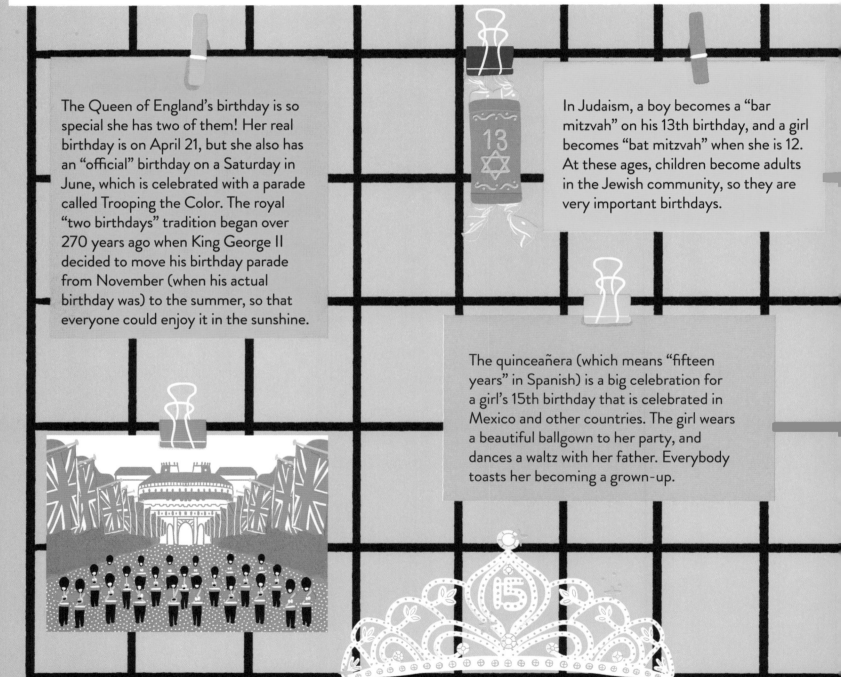

In China, Korea, and Vietnam, a child's first birthday is very important, and is celebrated with a special fortune-telling ceremony. The child is surrounded by objects, and whichever they pick up first supposedly predicts their future—choosing a book, for example, means they will be good at learning things, while picking up money means they will be rich! The tradition is hundreds of years old.

When you're a teenager, certain birthdays are a big deal, because they allow you to do important things for the first time, such as vote in elections. These important birthdays are different in different countries. In the UK, for instance, you're allowed to get a part-time job when you turn 14, drive a car at 17, and vote at 18. Which would you most look forward to?

Max

Employee

The Queen

If you are born on February 29th, you only get to celebrate on your actual birthday every four years. That's because February 29th only exists on leap years, which happen every four years. Leap-year birthdays are so special that people born on that day have a special name—leaplings!

Everyone has to agree that a 100th birthday is pretty special, right? In the UK, people who turn 100 (called "centenarians") receive a telegram from the Queen!

February

29

HAVE YOU EVER HEARD OF AN "UNBIRTHDAY?"

Unbirthdays are all the days of the year when it's not your birthday! The word was made up by author Lewis Carroll in his book *Through the Looking-Glass* (the sequel to *Alice's Adventures in Wonderland*). Why don't you wish someone a Happy Unbirthday today?

RECORD-BREAKING

LONGEST BIRTHDAY

Everyone's birthday lasts for a day, which is 24 hours, right? Think again! In 2018, Paul Morgan managed to make his birthday last for twice as long—a whopping 48 hours—making it the world's longest birthday. He did it by hopping onto planes and crossing time zones. One of his flights, all the way from New Zealand to Los Angeles, California, took off at 10.45pm on the evening of his birthday and landed at 2pm in the afternoon—on the same day.

MOST BIRTHDAY CANDLES

The record for the most candles on a birthday cake is... 72,585. Can you imagine how gigantic the cake must have been to fit all those candles? The cake was made in 2016 by a team of a hundred people at the Sri Chinmoy Center in New York, USA. There were so many candles, they had to be lit using blowtorches and put out with fire extinguishers.

BIRTHDAYS

Some birthdays are so amazing and extraordinary they've won themselves a place in the record books. Here are some of them.

MOST EXPENSIVE BIRTHDAY CAKE

Money can't buy you everything, but it can buy you the world's most expensive birthday cake. In 2015, British designer Debbie Wingham made a birthday cake for the daughter of a mystery customer living in the United Arab Emirates. The cake, which was designed to look like a fashion runway, was over 6 feet long and took over 1,100 hours to make. It featured over 4,000 real diamonds and cost (wait for it) $75 million. Gulp.

MOST BIRTHDAYS

Frenchwoman Jeanne Louise Calment, the oldest person to have ever lived, holds the record for the most birthdays—she had 122 of them. Jeanne was born in the French town of Arles in 1875, before the lightbulb was invented, and died in 1997. She loved chocolate and rode a bicycle until she was 100.

Some animals have had even more birthdays than Jeanne. A giant tortoise called Jonathan is the oldest living land animal. He lives on the island of St Helena in the Atlantic Ocean, and is thought to be over 185 years old.

That's nothing, though, compared to the world's oldest recorded animal—an ocean clam nicknamed Ming. Ming was discovered in 2006 but was accidentally killed when he was put into a deep freezer. When the scientists counted the rings on his shell, they discovered he was 507 years old—now THAT'S a lot of birthdays.

Can you think of any birthday records YOU would like to break? The biggest-ever birthday cake? The most birthday candles blown out in one puff? The youngest person ever to have a birthday in space? The most birthday balloons blown up in a minute? Who knows, maybe one day your birthday might end up in the record books.

In South Korea, birthdays sometimes start with a bowl of *miyeok guk*, or seaweed soup. It's known as "birthday soup," because it is traditionally eaten by new mothers after they have had a baby. Today people eat it on their birthdays to thank their mothers. Aw!

The birthday child gets to help decorate their own cake in Denmark. The **Kagemand (Cake man)** or **Kagekone (Cake Woman)** is a cake made out of dough, shaped like a boy or a girl, and decorated with icing and lots of candy—the more colorful it looks, the better. Traditionally, the birthday child cuts the head off the cake person while everyone around them screams.

BIRTHDAY FOOD

A traditional birthday breakfast in parts of Ghana is *oto*—mashed yams served with hard-boiled eggs. Family and friends are often invited to come and share the breakfast with the birthday boy or girl.

In India, Bengali families celebrate birthdays with **payesh**, a sweet rice pudding dish that is made for special occasions. Payesh is traditionally the very first food that babies eat.

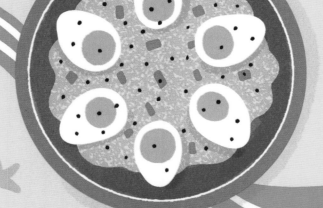

In China, people often celebrate their birthday with a bowl of **longevity noodles**. "Longevity" means "long life," and this is symbolized by the long lengths of the noodles—the idea is to eat them without breaking them, so that you will supposedly live for a long time. It is thought that the tradition of longevity noodles in China goes back over a thousand years.

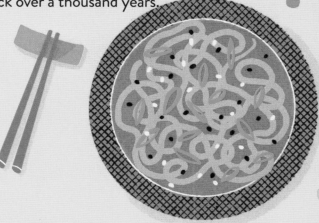

Fairy bread has been a popular birthday food in Australia for almost a hundred years. The recipe is very simple—white bread spread with butter, covered with masses of colorful sugar sprinkles. What's not to like?

One of the many, many brilliant things about birthdays is the yummy food! For many people, birthday food means birthday cake. But all sorts of other delicious things are eaten around the world on birthdays too.

Multi-storey sandwiches called **sandwiches de miga** are a popular party snack in Argentina. They are made using two or more slices of very thin white bread, layered with slices of ham, cheese, or other tasty fillings.

Turn to page 38 to find out how to make brigadeiros, a traditional Brazilian birthday treat.

I'M AS OLD AS A...

5 *kangaroo rat*
loveable and mischievous

Arctic fox
clever and brave
6

7 *bee hummingbird*
lively and energetic

8 *red panda*
gentle and shy

20
emperor penguin
determined and resilient

19
black-and-white ruffed lemur
high-spirited and boisterous

18
spotted owl
wise and perceptive

17
otter
playful and energetic

30 *Komodo dragon*
strong and courageous

40 *black swan*
elegant and unruffled

bottlenose dolphin
smart and fun-loving
50

60 *elephant*
intelligent and loving

Which animal do you share your age with? Look up your age below, and discover which animal lives for the same number of years. Do you know anyone who's as old and crinkly as a giant tortoise?

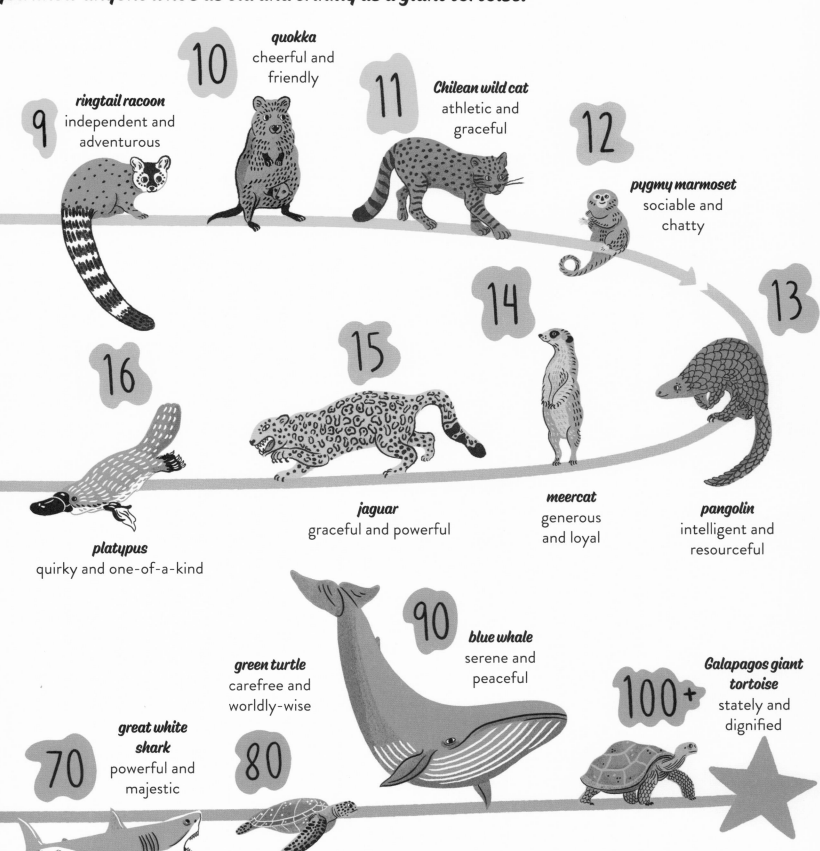

9 ringtail racoon
independent and adventurous

10 quokka
cheerful and friendly

11 Chilean wild cat
athletic and graceful

12 pygmy marmoset
sociable and chatty

13 pangolin
intelligent and resourceful

14 meercat
generous and loyal

15 jaguar
graceful and powerful

16 platypus
quirky and one-of-a-kind

70 great white shark
powerful and majestic

80 green turtle
carefree and worldly-wise

90 blue whale
serene and peaceful

100+ Galapagos giant tortoise
stately and dignified

A big thank you to my daughter, Mia, for her brilliant ideas and invaluable help testing out all the activities in this book. - C.S.

To my partner, Brian, thank you for supporting me through this process of illustrating my first book.
I cannot thank my family enough for their endless love & encouragement.
And a big thanks to my friends who cheered me on! -A.C.

Brimming with creative inspiration, how-to projects, and useful information to enrich your everyday life, Quarto Knows is a favorite destination for those pursuing their interests and passions. Visit our site and dig deeper with our books into your area of interest: Quarto Creates, Quarto Cooks, Quarto Homes, Quarto Lives, Quarto Drives, Quarto Explores, Quarto Gifts, or Quarto Kids.

Text © 2020 Claire Saunders. Illustrations © 2020 Alison Czinkota.
First published in 2021 by Frances Lincoln Children's Books, an imprint of The Quarto Group.
100 Cummings Center, Suite 265D, Beverly, MA 01915 USA.
T +1 978-282-9590 F +1 978-283-2742 www.QuartoKnows.com
The right of Claire Saunders to be identified as the author and Alison Czinkota to be identified as the illustrator of this work has been asserted by them in accordance with the Copyright, Designs and Patents Act, 1988 (United Kingdom).
A catalogue record for this book is available from the British Library.
ISBN 978-0-7112-5879-2
The illustrations were created digitally
Set in Suti and Brandon Grotesque
Published by Georgia Amson-Bradshaw
Designed by Karissa Santos
Edited by Lucy Brownridge
Production by Dawn Cameron

Manufactured in Guangdong, China EB042021
9 8 7 6 5 4 3 2